M000267435

New Directions for
Higher Education

Martin Kramer and
Betsy Barefoot
CO-EDITORS-IN-CHIEF

Disability Services and Campus Dynamics

Wendy S. Harbour
Joseph W. Madaus
EDITORS

Number 154 • Summer 2011
Jossey-Bass
San Francisco

DISABILITY SERVICES AND CAMPUS DYNAMICS
Wendy S. Harbour and Joseph W. Madaus
New Directions for Higher Education, no. 154
Martin Kramer, Betsy Barefoot, Co-Editors-in-Chief

Microfilm copies of issues and articles are available in 16mm and 35mm, as well as microfiche in 105mm, through University Microfilms Inc., 300 North Zeeb Road, Ann Arbor, MI 48106-1346.

NEW DIRECTIONS FOR HIGHER EDUCATION (ISSN 0271-0560, electronic ISSN 1536-0741) is part of The Jossey-Bass Higher and Adult Education Series and is published quarterly by Wiley Subscription Services, Inc., A Wiley Company, at Jossey-Bass, 989 Market Street, San Francisco, CA 94103-1741. Periodicals Postage Paid at San Francisco, California, and at additional mailing offices. POSTMASTER: Send address changes to New Directions for Higher Education, Jossey-Bass, 989 Market Street, San Francisco, CA 94103-1741.

New Directions for Higher Education is indexed in Current Index to Journals in Education (ERIC); Higher Education Abstracts.

SUBSCRIPTIONS cost $89 for individuals and $259 for institutions, agencies, and libraries. See ordering information page at end of journal.

EDITORIAL CORRESPONDENCE should be sent to the Co-Editors-in-Chief, Martin Kramer, 2807 Shasta Road, Berkeley, CA 94708-2011 and Betsy Barefoot, Gardner Institute, Box 72, Brevard, NC 28712.

Cover photograph © Digital Vision

www.josseybass.com

CONTENTS

EDITORS' NOTES

The second National Longitudinal Transition Study noted that the number of high school students with disabilities who are attending college has more than doubled since the 1980s (Wagner et al. 2005), and roughly 11 percent of college students are now identified as having disabilities (National Center for Education Statistics 2009). As several authors in this volume observe, the diversity of these students and the complexity of their disabilities are increasing over time. With greater inclusion occurring in K–12 education, the media, and society in general, a college education is becoming a goal for more people with disabilities. It is also a legitimate way to improve employment outcomes in a difficult economy, where only 18 percent of people with disabilities are employed (U.S. Bureau of Labor Statistics 2010). Similarly, as more students with disabilities graduate, they are joining the ranks of staff and faculty in higher education, meaning that disability services is not just for students anymore.

Thus history repeats itself—as each wave of students with disabilities breaks ground in higher education, colleges and universities adjust accordingly, with the federal government mandating better access and services through legislation. Administrators and faculty are now seeing a new generation of people with disabilities on campus. They arrive in higher education with knowledge that the law is on their side, ready to learn or work on any campus that is right for them, whether or not the campus itself is ready. Students with a variety of disabilities who have traditionally been excluded from higher education (e.g., students with intellectual disabilities, students with significant psychiatric disabilities) are knocking on the door of higher education, wondering why that door is not accessible. In response, campuses are turning to disability services for guidance on legal compliance, reasonable accommodations, classroom instruction issues, and strategies to improve the campus climate. This *New Directions* volume examines what disability services may have to offer, and how campuses and disability services professionals may need to collaborate or expand traditional notions of disability and disability services.

This volume is divided into four sections. In the first chapter, Joseph W. Madaus provides an introduction and overview of the field of disability services, explaining how it developed as a profession. The chapter provides useful definitions of disability services, as well as background and context for other chapters.

The second section continues to define disability services, complicating views of what disability services may provide to campuses. In chapter 2, Donna M. Korbel, Jennifer H. Lucia, Christine M. Wenzel, and Bryanna G. Anderson from the University of Connecticut explain how collaboration with other units on their campus has improved disability services' outreach and services to students, with creative ideas for reaching prospective and

NEW DIRECTIONS FOR HIGHER EDUCATION, no. 154, Summer 2011   © Wiley Periodicals, Inc.
Published online in Wiley Online Library (wileyonlinelibrary.com) • DOI:10.1002/he.428

first-year students in particular. Then Rebecca C. Cory explains some basic procedures and terminology related to disability services, including the process for determining reasonable accommodations. She further encourages campus administrators and faculty to not only consider legal mandates, but also ethical matters that may go beyond compliance. In chapter 4, Dave Edyburn provides an additional example of this "beyond compliance" attitude, explaining how technology can enhance service provision and instruction, creating campuses that are universally designed for diverse learners, including students with disabilities. Addressing the common assumption that disability services is only for students, Dave Fuecker and Wendy S. Harbour use chapter 5 to explain how the disability services office at the University of Minnesota is also serving faculty and staff. Serving not only employees with disabilities and chronic illnesses, the office also handles workers' compensation and insurance-related cases, centralizing services in one location. For campuses that need to expand or enhance services, the authors in this second section offer creative and varied recommendations.

The third section examines legal compliance in greater detail. In chapter 6, Salome Heyward discusses the Americans with Disabilities Act Amendments, students with psychiatric disabilities, and federal interest in accessible campus technology. Analyzing these issues using recent legislation and court cases, Heyward shows how campuses must continually respond to legal compliance—an ongoing journey rather than an end point. Anne Lundquist and Allan Shackelford take a similar approach in chapter 7. They also recommend that campuses examine their compliance with the law carefully, focusing on the development of risk management policies that are consistent with the needs of students, faculty, staff, and the institution as a whole. Taken together, these authors guide campuses toward more thoughtful proactive compliance.

Providing a counterpoint to legalities, the final section takes a more philosophical approach, looking at the bigger picture of disability itself, and how that relates to disability services. In chapter 8, Wanda M. Hadley considers how students with disabilities may change over the course of their college career, maturing in their identity as students with disabilities and in the ways they use services. In chapter 9, Robert A. Stodden, Steven E. Brown, and Kelly Roberts explain their research of campus assessment tools, and strategies for learning about campus climate for students, faculty, and staff with disabilities. They also make recommendations about how the results of these assessments may inform policies and programs in disability services and across campus. Sharing his perspective as a pioneer in his field, the final chapter by Steven J. Taylor comes from a Disability Studies perspective. Like African American Studies, Women's Studies, Queer Studies, and other fields that examine issues of oppression, difference, and societal norms, Disability Studies uses disability as a lens for looking at culture, society, and politics. It can also turn its lens on disability services and higher education, providing insights into how disability is defined on campus. These chapters start with an assumption of disability as part of campus diversity, and then ask how the campus can be more welcoming of this diversity.

This volume illustrates how the nascent field of disability services is still growing, and how even definitions of disability services change depending on one's perspective. In editing this volume, we hoped to provide a snapshot of the field in its current context, addressing what administrators may need to know in addressing disability-related needs of their institutions (we occasionally referred to this volume as "Disability Services 101"). We are painfully aware that some questions will not be addressed in this issue; because the field is so new, many gaps exist in research and commentary about disability services, especially with traditionally demarcated groups (e.g., students of color who also have disabilities). We hope this volume provides a reference point for determining what those gaps may be, as well as inspiration for campuses and researchers to address them with innovative approaches.

We thank the authors of these chapters for their contributions to an ongoing dialogue about disability services and disability on campus. We dedicate this volume to students, faculty, and staff with disabilities who push the field forward by expecting the ivory tower to be welcoming and accessible. We also dedicate it to disability services professionals and other allies who share the same vision for higher education and are working to make it a reality.

References

National Center for Education Statistics. 2009. "Number and Percentage Distribution of Students Enrolled in Postsecondary Institutions, by Level, Disability Status, and Selected Student and Characteristics: 2003–04 and 2007–08." *Digest of Education Statistics.* Accessed July 20, 2010. http://nces.ed.gov/programs/digest/d09/tables /dt09_231.asp.

U.S. Bureau of Labor Statistics. "Employment Situation Summary." Washington, DC: U.S. Bureau of Labor Statistics, December 10, 2010. Accessed December 20, 2010. http://www.bls.gov/news.release/empsit.nr0.htm.

Wagner, M., Newman, L., Cameto, R., and Levine, P. 2005. "Changes Over Time in the Early Postschool Outcomes of Youth with Disabilities: A Report of Findings from the National Longitudinal Transition Study (NLTS) and the National Longitudinal Transition Study-2 (NLTS2)." Menlo Park, CA: SRI International.

Wendy S. Harbour
Joseph W. Madaus
Editors

WENDY S. HARBOUR *is the Lawrence B. Taishoff Professor of Inclusive Education at Syracuse University, where she directs the Taishoff Center for Inclusive Higher Education.*

JOSEPH W. MADAUS *is the Co-Director of the Center on Postsecondary Education and Disability and is an Associate Professor in the Department of Educational Psychology at the University of Connecticut.*

1

In parallel with educational, social, technological, and legal changes in higher education, disability services has evolved rapidly, with professionals addressing increasingly complex issues on their campuses.

The History of Disability Services in Higher Education

Joseph W. Madaus

In 2002, Brinckerhoff, McGuire, and Shaw observed that the field of postsecondary education and disability services had "moved through its adolescence and was embarking on adulthood" (xiii). Indeed, the field had undergone rapid expansion nationwide in the prior thirty years and grew into a full-fledged profession within higher education (Jarrow 1997). Now nearly a decade later, the field serves an estimated 11 percent of all students in higher education (National Center for Education Statistics 2009). However, the development of this sector of higher education is largely unrecognized in books covering both the history of higher education, and disability rights and history. This article will provide an overview of some of the seminal events in the development of postsecondary disability services, and will highlight some emerging trends that may influence services in the coming years.

Early Efforts

In 1864, with congressional approval, President Lincoln signed into law a bill authorizing the establishment of a college division at the Columbia Institution for the Deaf and Dumb. Under the directorship of Edward Miner Gallaudet, the National Deaf-Mute College enrolled its first student in the fall of 1864, and by 1866, had twenty-five students (including two women) from thirteen states and the District of Columbia (Gallaudet 1983). The first class graduated in 1869, and according to Gallaudet's personal account, "the graduation of the first bachelors of arts in a college for the deaf-mutes, from what could be justly claimed to be a regular collegiate course of study, excited unusual interest in the educational world" (100).

NEW DIRECTIONS FOR HIGHER EDUCATION, no. 154, Summer 2011 © Wiley Periodicals, Inc.
Published online in Wiley Online Library (wileyonlinelibrary.com) • DOI:10.1002/he.429

In 1894, in response to "dislike of the presence of the words deaf-mute in the name of the college" (Gallaudet 1983, 188), the college division was renamed Gallaudet College, in honor of E. M. Gallaudet's father, Thomas Hopkins Gallaudet. Authorized by Congress as a university in 1986, Gallaudet University now offers undergraduate degrees in 40 majors, as well as graduate degrees (History of Gallaudet University 2010) and remains the only liberal arts university in the world for the deaf (Burch 2001).

Beyond Gallaudet, examples of individuals with disabilities in higher education existed, such as Helen Keller's attendance at Radcliffe College from 1900 to 1905 (Nielsen 2001) but were largely isolated. Changes began to occur at the end of World War I and, more significantly, at the end of World War II.

Early to Mid-Twentieth Century

After World War I, the federal government passed the Vocational Rehabilitation Act of 1918, which led to educational assistance for some veterans with disabilities (Chatterjee and Mitra 1998). College study occurred in such areas as industry, trade, and agriculture. Professional training was also provided for some veterans with prior college experience (Gelber 2005). Another notable program was established at the Ohio Mechanics Institute (OMI) in Cincinnati, which provided services to over 400 veterans with disabilities. In conjunction with a veterans group at the University of Cincinnati, the OMI students formed the Disabled American Veterans, which continues to be active today (Disabled American Veterans 1995).

In 1944, Congress passed the Serviceman's Readjustment Act of 1944, more commonly known as the GI Bill of Rights. This legislation provided $500 per year of educational expenses to qualified veterans depending on length of service at approved institutions (Strom 1950). This legislation resulted in an immediate impact on college campuses. Strom (1950) noted that "after the formal signing of the surrender papers, the hue and cry began all over the world to get the men home . . . this accelerated demobilization program necessarily resulted in an unexpected upsurge in applications for college training" (24). By 1946, veterans constituted 52 percent of the total college population in the United States, with over $2 billion in federal funds being expended annually (Strom 1950).

This influx of veterans resulted in a corresponding increase in students with disabilities enrolling in college. A study of veterans with disabilities in higher education commissioned by the American Council on Education (ACE), noted:

> For the first time in the history of American higher education, student bodies are composed of a sizable number of disabled veterans, ranging in types of disability from minor ailments to almost total physical disability. These disabled veterans, as well as other handicapped students, required, in many

instances, particular services to enable them to achieve maximum progress in academic work. (Strom 1950, 38)

Results of the ACE study (with 453 responses from 595 member institutions) described the presenting disabilities, such as those students who were "leg and arm amputees, those with spinal and back injuries, those with diseases such as malaria and tuberculosis, the deafened and the blinded, and those with psychoneurotic disabilities" (Strom 1950, 39). The report also provided examples of services provided to veterans with disabilities, many of which are common today. These were broken into three broad areas: transportation facilities (e.g., special elevator privileges, parking privileges, guides to take the blind to classes, extra stair railings, ramps into buildings); housing facilities (e.g., first-floor rooms, homes close to campus, permission to live in dorms throughout college plan of study); and classroom facilities (e.g., scheduling classes in locations that minimize distance to travel, provision of readers and notetakers, priority seating and course registration) (Strom, 1950).

These programs emerged throughout the country, but were most often near veteran's hospitals. A story in a 1947 edition of *Phi Delta Kappan* (Atkinson 1947) explained that "an interesting and unusual educational program for handicapped students in the United States is currently being carried out at the University of California, Los Angeles. Here, eighteen veteran students in wheelchairs live, study, go to classes, and otherwise maintain a normal student existence" (295). This program was initially conducted with the Birmingham Veterans Hospital in Van Nuys. Likewise, a program was initiated at the University of Illinois in 1947 when a VA Hospital in Galesburg became a satellite campus and students with disabilities were among those enrolled. When the campus closed, a group of students with disabilities self-advocated to gain "experimental" enrollment states at the main campus in Urbana-Champaign. Through active advocacy, this group became firmly established on the campus (History of Disability Services at the University of Illinois 2008; Nugent 1978). Other examples cited in the literature included the City College of the City University of New York (Condon 1951, 1962) and the University of Minnesota (Berdie 1955).

However, discrimination on the basis of disability still existed, such as the case of a student who attempted to return to his studies after war service. However, the administration of his university was "convinced that a paraplegic simply couldn't do the work." With the advocacy of faculty, the student was admitted and eventually earned a PhD (Rusk 1977, as cited in Fleischer and James 2001). Nugent (1978) summarized the perception of many faculty and administrators in colleges across the nation in 1948, stating that many felt "to include severely handicapped students in regular college programs would be a waste of time and effort" and "most felt there was little reason to believe that seriously disabled people would be able to succeed in college or be able to use their schooling after graduation" (12). Likewise, a study of two-year colleges by Brooks and Brooks (1962) indicated that schools near Veterans' Hospitals were providing services to students with physical disabilities, but other institutions reported not accepting students because the campus was not accessible.

Although such discrimination existed, the ACE report made a clear statement to higher education, noting that "physical disability is not, and should not be an insurmountable handicap to the successful achievement of the benefits of a college career" (Strom 1950, 47). It further discussed the economic importance of such programs, clearly stating, "if the country is to capitalize on the total talent reserve in its young people, then the resources of this group must not be overlooked" (46).

Programs continued to develop in the aftermath of World War II and the Korean War. Condon (1957) conducted a "national canvas of special facilities for the physically handicapped in colleges and universities" (579) and, in a summary paper published in 1962, described a range of services being offered nationwide. These included notification and training for instructors related to student needs, priority seating, texts on tape, the recording of lectures, and examinations administered in a separate location. Condon also described what could be considered a forerunner of today's trends in distance education, a program at Boston University for "homebound" students who are taught by tutors, by telephone, and by tape recorders.

Another early pioneer in the area of services for students with disabilities was Herbert Rusalem. In 1962, Rusalem wrote:

> Physically handicapped college students requiring one or more special educational services are no longer a rarity on the American campus. Having the same goals as other students, they are enrolling in increasing numbers, encouraged by better public and private school preparation, improved rehabilitation services, the availability of scholarship funds, and a changing attitude toward disabled persons in our society. Since these sources of encouragement will probably become more influential in the future, in seems likely that the problems of educating the physically handicapped student will be receiving increasing attention. (161)

While advocating for increased and improved services, Rusalem also clearly noted that the "basic assumption in accepting the disabled student into a college is that, with certain possible modifications in procedure, he can attain stated levels of performance" (162–163) and thus "college-wide standards should be maintained" (162). These two statements remain key tenants in today's disability services.

The 1970s to 2000

Rusalem's prediction in 1962 of increasing numbers of students with disabilities accessing higher education proved to be prescient. While veterans with disabilities had a profound impact on the development of early disability services (Madaus et al. 2009), the civil rights movement and legislation, as well as education legislation at the K–12 level, served as a catalyst for an era of greatly expanded services. Until the 1960s, the majority of discussion in the professional disability literature related to physical disabilities. However, in 1963, the term *learning disability* (LD) was used by Dr. Samuel Kirk (Hallahan and Mercer 2001), and by 1968, this term was designated by the federal government as a category of disability in the K–12 system (Kavale 2001). Shortly thereafter, services specific for students with hidden disabilities such as LD were developed in public schools, and the number of students identified with such disabilities dramatically increased, rising to constitute more than half of all students with disabilities in just over 20 years (Hallahan and Mercer 2001).

In 1975, Congress passed the Education of All Handicapped Children Act (P.L. 94–142). This legislation required that special education services be provided to students with disabilities. Also required were individualized education programs based on periodic assessments, and the development of individualized goals. Subsequent amendments to the act included a specific focus on planning for the transition to adult life, including postsecondary education. Now more than thirty-five years old, the legislation serves more than six million students aged six to twenty-one annually (U.S. Department of Education 2006), and has consequently resulted in more students with disabilities becoming qualified to pursue higher education.

However, it was another piece of federal legislation that was essential in increasing access to postsecondary education for students with disabilities. Within the wording of the Vocational Rehabilitation Act of 1973 was the following language:

> No otherwise qualified handicapped individual in the United States shall, solely by reason of his handicap, be excluded from participation in, be denied the benefits of, or be subjected to discrimination under any program or activity receiving Federal financial assistance.

Moreover, Section E of Section 504 specifically related to postsecondary education, and required institutions, both public and private, to consider the applications of qualified students with disabilities and to implement necessary accommodations and auxiliary aids for students with disabilities. Based on the language of other civil rights laws (Feldblum 1996), the regulations for Section 504 were signed into law in 1977. Fears about the costs of implementing the regulations were reflected in a 1977 article in the *Chronicle of Higher Education* entitled "Providing Access for the Disabled: It Won't Be Cheap or Easy" (Fields 1977, 4). Bailey (1979) described the ensuing reaction as the "panic period" (88) and noted that some colleges feared closure because of costs related to compliance.

While these predictions did not hold true, Section 504 had a significant impact on access to postsecondary education for students with disabilities. It required private institutions to consider the applications of these students, improved access to campus programs and facilities, addressed discrimination on the basis of a disability, and ended the practice of counseling students with disabilities into more restrictive majors and careers (Bailey 1979; Scales 1986). The subsequent passage of the Americans with Disabilities Act (ADA) in 1990 led to additional program development and student access to higher education, and heightened public awareness of disability rights. Now twenty years old, the ADA was recently reauthorized with new language that contains some significant implications for postsecondary institutions to carefully consider (see Heyward, this volume).

The 1990s also saw the advancement of self-determination theory in higher education disability services. Based on the idea of helping an individual with a disability to engage in "goal directed, self-regulated, autonomous behavior" with an understanding of one's strengths and limitations (Field et al. 1998, 115), self-determination has been proven to be an essential component of successful transition to higher education and student success once enrolled. The concept of universal design (UD), originally rooted in architecture, began to emerge in college instruction at the turn of the century as a means to reach the needs of a broad range of learners, including those with disabilities. Edyburn (this volume) describes UD in more detail, as well as its use in higher education instruction.

The rapid growth in student access and consequent program development can be measured in a variety of ways. Since 1966, the Cooperative Institutional Research Program (CIRP) Freshman Survey has been administered to incoming first-year students at over 1,200 American colleges and universities, collecting data on student characteristics, values, and attitudes (Wyer 2007). In 1978, a question was added to the survey related to the existence of a handicapping condition, and less than 3 percent of the respondents reported having a disability (Henderson 1999). By the 2007–2008 academic year, students with disabilities represented 11 percent of all undergraduate students (National Center for Education Statistics 2009). The types of disabilities reported also changed significantly. In the 1988 CIRP Freshman Survey, the largest category of student disabilities was students with blindness or a visual impairment (Henderson 1999). In the 2008 academic year, students with learning disabilities made up 3.3 percent of all college freshmen (Pryor et al. 2008).

The growth and firm establishment of disability services as a profession in higher education also became evident in this time period. In 1977, the "Disabled Students on American Campuses: Services and State of the Art" conference, funded by the Federal Bureau of Education for the Handicapped, was held at Wright State University (Marx and Hall 1977, 1978). From this conference, a group of 32 attendees formed the Association on Handicapped Student Service Programs in Postsecondary Education (Scales

1986). The organization was renamed the Association on Higher Education And Disability (AHEAD) in 1992 and by 2010 had over 2,500 members from eleven countries (Association on Higher Education And Disability 2010). A study of national disability service programs in 1996 indicated that 11 percent were in existence prior to the passage of Section 504, while 89 percent were developed after the regulations were passed (Madaus 1996). By the end of the 1990s, AHEAD had established Program Standards as well as Professional Standards and a Code of Ethics for practitioners (see http://www.ahead.org/resources).

Backlash

As this progress was occurring, a backlash against services for students with disabilities emerged (Gephart 1997; Jarrow 1997; Madaus 2000). As Gephart described, this was particularly true in the area of learning disabilities, where issues that had "simmered below the surface for years" finally "boiled over" (I-1). Significant court cases emerged in both the higher education and testing agency arena (see, e.g., *Guckenberger v. Boston University*, *Bartlett v. New York State Board of Law Examiners*, and *Price v. National Board of Medical Examiners*) and in the employment arena (see, e.g., *Toyota Motor Manufacturing, Kentucky, Inc. v. Williams*, *Sutton v. United Airlines*, *Murphy v. United States Parcel Service*), bringing attention to a range of issues related to documentation of disabilities, reasonable accommodations, definitions of "major life activities," and the impact of mitigating measures on the impact of a disability (Gephart 1998; Madaus 2000). In general, these court rulings led to more restrictive interpretation of the ADA regulations, a point that was specifically addressed by Congress in 2008 by the Americans with Disabilities Act Amendments Act (ADAAA) (Shaw et al. 2010).

The Current Landscape and Emerging Issues

Legislation. In 2009, Congress passed the ADAAA specifically to address some of the limitations imposed by the courts on the ADA. Included was clear language related to the definition of *disability,* expanded examples of what constitutes a disabling condition, and the clarification of impact of mitigating measures in making eligibility determinations. In this volume, Heyward describes many of the key issues facing colleges and universities in relation to the enactment of this legislation. Clearly, how the courts and the Office for Civil Rights interpret these regulations will need to be played out over the next decade.

New Populations. While the number of students with LD has grown dramatically over the past twenty-five years, students with different disability types are now increasing exponentially. These conditions will place new demands on institutions and, consequently, require new considerations related to service delivery and policy (U.S. Government Accountability

Office 2009). For example, the number of students with psychological/psychiatric disabilities has increased significantly over the past decade. According to some data sets, these students are now the largest group of students with disabilities on campus (U.S. Government Accountability Office 2009). Although many of these cases are mild and require only minimal support, others are more significant and may require services that exceed what existing campus counseling centers can provide (U.S. Government Accountability Office 2009). Although smaller, the number of students on college campuses with autism spectrum disorders (including those with Asperger's syndrome) is increasing and requires consideration (U.S. Government Accountability Office 2009). The most recent amendments to the Higher Education Opportunity Act provide funding for the development and enhancement of programs for students with intellectual disabilities (formerly labeled as having "mental retardation"), and therefore new challenges for institutions to consider (U.S. Government Accountability Office 2009).

Another emerging population requiring campuswide coordination is veterans with disabilities returning to college after service in Operation Iraqi Freedom and Operation Enduring Freedom (U.S. Government Accountability Office 2009). As a result of the Post-9/11 Veterans Educational Assistance Act of 2008 (also known as the New GI Bill), it is estimated that over two million veterans will enroll in higher education (ACE 2008) and that as many as 25 percent of these students will have hidden disabilities, such as traumatic brain injury, posttraumatic stress disorder, and other emotional disabilities (Rand Center for Military Health Policy Research 2008). These veterans may have different perspectives on disability than traditional students, may be less willing to self-disclose, and, if they so choose, may present documentation that does not meet traditional institutional requirements. The definition of *disability* used by the military may also not match that used by postsecondary institutions. As a result, this segment of students with disabilities may not receive the services needed to fully access their education (Madaus, Miller, and Vance 2009). Additionally, postsecondary institutions should be aware that the Office of Civil Rights launched a "Wounded Warriors Initiative" that is designed to not only support veterans with disabilities in higher education, but also to "encourage institutions to adopt innovative approaches to serve this important population" (Monroe 2008, 3). Interested readers are referred to a special issue of the *Journal of Postsecondary Education and Disability* (2009, Volume 22, Number 1) that outlines many of the specific issues facing colleges in this regard, and highlights several innovative programs related to serving these students.

Technology. The impact of technology continues to be an enigma for colleges in relation to students with disabilities. While assistive technology continues to develop to provide new access to students (e.g., digital textbooks, smartpens, smartphones), other advances in technology can create different access issues for students with disabilities. For example, although enrollment in online classes has grown exponentially over the past five years

(Allen and Seaman 2010), the access needs of students with learning disabilities have been virtually ignored in the development and implementation of these courses (Madaus, Banerjee, and McKeown in press). Ironically, it is thought that advances in assistive technology (AT) may be the cause of this, as web and course designers believe that AT can take care of most access needs (Keeler and Horney 2007). Furthermore, although Section 508 of the Rehabilitation Act mandates that institutional websites be accessible, research indicates that many are not (Erickson et al. 2009).

Summary

Over the past twenty-five years, the field of postsecondary disability services has moved from a fledgling aspect of the higher education enterprise to an established profession. Simultaneously, college campuses are faced with new issues related to providing services for an increasingly diverse student body, including ensuring access to evolving technologies, to quality instruction, and to appropriate support services. Disability service professionals can provide a valuable resource to campus administrations in the development and evolution of such services, but moreover, stand poised to increasingly serve in a campus leadership role in such endeavors.

References

Allen, I. E., and J. Seaman. 2010, January. "Learning on Demand: Online Education in the United States, 2009." Babson Park, MA: Babson Survey Research Group and the Sloan Consortium.

American Council on Education (ACE). 2008, November. "Serving Those Who Serve: Higher Education and America's Veterans." Accessed August 16, 2010. http://www.acenet .edu/Content/NavigationMenu/ProgramsServices/MilitaryPMilitar /serving/Veterans _Issue_Brief_1108.pdf.

Association on Higher Education And Disability. 2010. "About AHEAD, 2010." Accessed August 5, 2010. http://ahead.org.about.

Atkinson, B. H. 1947. "Students in Wheelchairs." *Phi Delta Kappan* 24: 295–97.

Bailey, C. W. 1979. "Adapting to the Revolution of Equal Opportunity of the Handicapped." In *Assuring Access for the Handicapped,* edited by M. R. Redden. New Directions for Higher Education, no. 25. San Francisco: Jossey-Bass.

Berdie, R. 1955. "Counseling for Physically Disabled Students." *Journal of Higher Education* 26: 475–78.

Brinckerhoff, L. C., J. M. McGuire, and S. F. Shaw. 2002. *Postsecondary Education and Transition for Students with Learning Disabilities,* 2nd ed. Austin, TX: PRO-ED Inc.

Brooks, S., and R. H. Brooks. 1962. "Handicapped Students and the California Two-Year College." *Junior College Journal* 33 (1): 50–56.

Burch, S. 2001. "Reading Between the Signs: Defending Deaf Culture in Early Twentieth-Century America." In *The New Disability History*, edited by P. K. Longmore and L. Umansky. New York: New York University Press.

Chatterjee, L., and M. Mitra. 1998. "Evolution of Federal and State Policies for Persons with Disability in the United States: Efficiency and Welfare Impacts." *Annals of Regional Science* 32: 347–65.

Condon, M. E. 1951. "This College Concentrates on Helping the Handicapped Student." *Journal of Rehabilitation* 12 (3): 14–16.

———1957. "A Survey of Special Facilities for the Physically Handicapped in the Colleges. *Personnel and Guidance Journal* 35 (9): 579–83.

———1962. "The Facilitation of the Education of the Physically Disabled College Student." *Rehabilitation Literature* 23 (9): 266–74.

Disabled American Veterans. 1995, August. "Wars and Scars, Compassion and Service: A Diamond Anniversary of the Disabled American Veteran." *DAV Magazine* 37: Special Insert.

Erickson, W., S. Trerise, S. VanLooy, C. Lee, and S. Bruyere. 2009. "Web Accessibility Policies and Practices at American Community Colleges." *Community College Journal of Research Practice* 33 (5): 403–14.

Feldblum, C. R. 1996. "The (R)evolution of Physical Disability Antidiscrimination Law: 1976–1996." *Mental and Physical Disability Law Reporter* 5: 613–21.

Field, S., J. Martin, R. Miller, M. Ward, and M. Wehmeyer. 1998. "Self-Determination for Persons with Disabilities: A Position Statement of the Division on Career Development and Transition." *Career Development for Exceptional Individuals* 21 (2): 113–28.

Fields, C. M. 1977, May 31. "Providing Access for the Disabled: It Won't Be Cheap or Easy." *Chronicle of Higher Education* 4–5.

Fleischer, D. Z., and F. James. 2001. *The Disability Rights Movement: From Charity to Confrontation.* Philadelphia: Temple University Press.

Gallaudet, E. M. 1983. *History of the College for the Deaf, 1857–1907.* Washington, DC: Gallaudet College Press.

Gelber, S. 2005. "A 'Hard-Boiled Order': The Reeducation of Disabled WWI Veterans in New York City." *Journal of Social History* 39 (1): 161–80.

Gephart, D. J. 1997. *Disability Compliance for Higher Education: 1997 Yearbook.* Horsham, PA: LRP Publications.

———1998. *Disability Compliance for Higher Education: 1998 Yearbook.* Horsham, PA: LRP Publications.

Hallahan, D. P., and C. D. Mercer. 2001. "Learning Disabilities: Historical Perspectives." *White Paper from the Learning Disabilities Summit.* Accessed August 16, 2010. http://ldsummit.air.org/download/Hallahan%20Final%2008–10–01.pdf.

Henderson, C. 1999. *College Freshmen with Disabilities: A Biennial Statistic Profile. Statistical Year 1998.* Washington, DC: American Council on Education, HEATH Resource Center.

History of Disability Services at the University of Illinois. 2008. Accessed August 16, 2010. http://www.disability.uiuc.edu/page.php?id=10.

History of Gallaudet University. 2010. Accessed August 5, 2010. http://aaweb.gallaudet.edu/About_Gallaudet/History_of_the_University.html.

Jarrow, J. 1997. "Why Do We Need Professional Standards?" *Journal of Postsecondary, Education and Disability* 12 (3): 5–7.

Kavale, K. A. 2001. "Discrepancy Models in the Identification of Learning Disability." *White Paper from the Learning Disabilities Summit.* Retrieved August 16, 2010. http://ldsummit.air.org/download/Kavale%20Final%2008–10–01.pdf.

Keeler, C. G., and M. Horney. 2007. "Online Course Designs: Are Special Needs Being Met?" *American Journal of Distance Education* 21 (2): 61–75.

Madaus, J. W. 1996. *Administration of Postsecondary Offices for Students with Disabilities: Perceptions of Essential Job Functions.* Doctoral Dissertation, University of Connecticut, Storrs.

———2000. "Services for College and University Students with Disabilities: A Historical Perspective." *Journal of Postsecondary Education and Disability* 14 (1): 4–21.

Madaus, J. W., M. Banerjee, and K. McKeown. In press. "Online and Blended Learning: The Opportunities and the Challenges for Students with Learning Disabilities and

Attention Deficit/Hyperactivity Disorder." *Learning Disabilities: A Multidisciplinary Journal.*

Madaus, J. W., W. K. Miller, and M. L. Vance. 2009. "Veterans with Disabilities in Postsecondary Education. *Journal of Postsecondary Education and Disability* 22 (1): 10–17.

Marx, P., and P. Hall. 1977, 1978. *Forward.* Paper presented at the Disabled Student on American Campuses: Services and State of the Art conference, Wright State University, Dayton, OH.

Monroe, S. J. 2008. *Dear Colleague Letter.* Washington, DC: United States Department of Education, Office for Civil Rights.

National Center for Education Statistics. 2009. "Number and Percentage Distribution of Students Enrolled in Postsecondary Institutions, by Level, Disability Status, and Selected Student and Characteristics: 2003–04 and 2007–08. *Digest of Education Statistics.* Accessed July 20, 2010. http://nces.ed.gov/programs/digest/d09/tables/dt09_231.asp.

Nielsen, K. 2001. "Helen Keller and the Politics of Civic Fitness." In *The New Disability History,* edited by P. K. Longmore and L. Umansky, 268–290. New York: New York University Press.

Nugent, T. J. 1978. "More Than Ramps and Braille." *American Education* 14 (7): 11–18.

Pryor, J. H., S. Hurtado, L. DeAngelo, J. Sharkness, L. C. Romero, W. S. Korn, and S. Tran. 2008. *The American Freshman: National Norms for Fall 2008.* Los Angeles: Higher Education Research Institute, University of California.

Rand Center for Military Health Policy Research. 2008, April. *Invisible Wounds: Mental Health and Cognitive Care Needs of America's Returning Veterans.* Accessed November 27, 2008. http://www.rand.org/pubs/research_briefs/RB9336.

Rusalem, H. 1962. "The Physically Handicapped Student and the College Faculty." *College and University* 37 (2): 161–67.

Scales, W. (1986). "Postsecondary Education for Disabled Students—Written Testimony." *AHSSPPE Bulletin* 4 (1): 20–32.

Shaw, S. F., W. R. Keenan, J. W. Madaus, and M. Banerjee. 2010. "Disability Documentation, the Americans with Disabilities Act Amendments Act, and the Summary of Performance: How Are They Linked? *Journal of Postsecondary Education* 22 (3): 142–150.

Strom, R. J. 1950. *The Disabled College Veteran of World War II.* Washington, DC: American Council on Education.

U.S. Department of Education. 2006. *28th Annual Report to Congress on the Implementation of the Individuals with Education Act, 2006,* 1. Accessed August 24, 2010. http://www2.ed.gov/about/reports/annual/osep/2006/parts-b-c/28th-vol-1.pdf.

U.S. Government Accountability Office. 2009. *Higher Education and Disability: Education Needs a Coordinated Approach to Improve its Assistance to Schools in Supporting Students.* Washington, DC: United States Government Accountability Office.

Wyer, K. 2007, April. "Today's College Freshmen Have Family Income 60% Above National Average, UCLA Survey Reveals." *UCLA News.* Accessed August 5, 2010. http://gseis.ucla.edu/heri/PDFs/PR_TRENDS_40YR.pdf.

Joseph W. Madaus is the Co-Director of the Center on Postsecondary Education and Disability and is an Associate Professor in the Department of Educational Psychology at the University of Connecticut.

2

Examples from the University of Connecticut demonstrate how outreach and services may require collaboration with campus and off-campus resources, particularly for students with disabilities transitioning from high school.

Collaboration Strategies to Facilitate Successful Transition of Students with Disabilities in a Changing Higher Education Environment

Donna M. Korbel, Jennifer H. Lucia, Christine M. Wenzel, Bryanna G. Anderson

According to the latest data available from the National Center for Education Statistics (NCES 2009), close to 11 percent of students enrolled in post-secondary education are students with disabilities. The 2008 reauthorization of the Americans with Disabilities Act, the Higher Education Opportunity Act of 2008 (HEOA), and the Post-9/11 Veterans Educational Assistance Act of 2008 all have the potential to further increase these numbers (Burke, Friedl, and Rigler 2010). Despite growing numbers, it is unlikely that most disability service (DS) offices have had a corresponding increase in staff to meet the demand. Depending on a variety of institutional variables (e.g., size of institution, public or private entity), many colleges and universities have given the responsibility of disability services to other departments on campus that are already stretched thin, such as health services, counseling centers, or the dean of students (Harbour 2008). In addition, the complexities of disabilities, including students with multiple chronic health conditions and severe psychiatric disorders, may necessitate more than just academic accommodations (see, e.g., Cory, this volume). Accommodations often need to go beyond the classroom and require the DS professional to collaborate and problem-solve with colleagues across campus in order to provide appropriate support.

DS offices today need to be resourceful, creative, and forward-thinking in order to meet the needs of college students with disabilities. A key strategy to meeting these needs is to develop relationships with colleagues across

NEW DIRECTIONS FOR HIGHER EDUCATION, no. 154, Summer 2011 © Wiley Periodicals, Inc.
Published online in Wiley Online Library (wileyonlinelibrary.com) • DOI:10.1002/he.430

17

the campus, in both Student and Academic Affairs (Whitt et al. 2008). The Center for Students with Disabilities (CSD) at the University of Connecticut has fostered and developed dozens of collaborative relationships with departments across campus. While the CSD is housed in the Division of Student Affairs, providing physical and programmatic access to students with disabilities is an institutional responsibility that can be accomplished only by building partnerships and creating a sense of shared ownership. This chapter will begin by describing some emerging populations of students requiring a coordinated and collaborative campus. Several initiatives and strategies employed by the CSD to foster collaborative relationships and better these populations will be presented, each of which could be replicated on other campuses.

Emerging Populations of Students with Disabilities

There are several emerging populations of students on campus who demonstrate the importance of collaboration between DS and other units. While not exhaustive, this list provides some examples for consideration.

Asperger's Syndrome. The National Institutes of Health (2010) estimates that two to six of every 1,000 American students are on the autism spectrum (which includes autism and Asperger's syndrome). While much is already known about students on the spectrum, there are several characteristics typical to this population that present important considerations for college and university personnel. Although each student on the spectrum presents differently, one of the defining characteristics of this population is their "qualitative impairment in social interaction" (American Psychiatric Association 2000, 59). As any Student Affairs professional can attest, college environments are highly social in nature, and, according to Farmour-Dougan, James, and McKinney (2000), a student's level of engagement is often tied in part to interactions and dealings with other students. Students with Asperger's may be highly intelligent but often miss, or misunderstand, nonverbal cues and the subtleties of language in social situations. Thus, interacting with peers, staff, and faculty can be a challenge and a source of anxiety and frustration (Wolf et al. 2009). In order to evade these feelings, students with Asperger's syndrome often become isolated and reluctant to ask for help, further exacerbating their social deficits and level of engagement. It is essential that DS personnel educate campus colleagues and assist with ongoing adjustment issues.

GLBTQ Students. Historically, students with disabilities who are gay, lesbian, bisexual, transgendered, or questioning (GLBTQ), have not been considered as a cohesive group; rather, they have been viewed as being part of one population or the other (Henry et al. 2010). This feeling of not belonging or "fitting in" with any particular group may lead to isolation, depression, anxiety, or even substance abuse (Dworkin 2000), and it is estimated that GLBTQ populations are almost 2.5 times more likely than heterosexuals to have had mental health disorders (National Alliance on Mental Illness

2009). Collaboration across campus units, particularly with GLBTQ, counseling, and residential life professionals can serve to create supportive and inclusive environments to address these issues in an informed manner taking into consideration the multiple cultural identities and perhaps enhancing their comfort and the frequency with which they access services.

Veterans. Colleges and universities should expect to serve approximately two million veterans returning from the conflicts in Afghanistan and Iraq (American Council on Education [ACE] 2008). Of these, approximately one-third report symptoms of a mental health or cognitive condition. From 2001 to the present, approximately 1.64 million American troops have been deployed to Afghanistan and Iraq for Operation Enduring Freedom (OEF) and Operation Iraqi Freedom (OIF) (Rand Center for Military Health Policy Research 2008). Eighty-five percent of veterans who were injured in these two conflicts survived due to improvements in body armor, coagulants, and the modern medical evacuation system. Although more soldiers are surviving, more veterans are also returning home having experienced physical or mental trauma. More specifically, 18.5 percent report posttraumatic stress disorder (PTSD) or depression, 19.5 percent report experiencing a traumatic brain injury (TBI), and 7 percent met the criteria for both PTSD and a TBI (Rand Center for Military Health Policy Research 2008). Substance abuse often is also an issue and occurs in approximately 50–85 percent of those diagnosed with PTSD (Coll et al. 2009).

Difficulty with readjusting to civilian life, managing new physical and mental conditions, and limited or no understanding of disability accommodations may be barriers to veterans who are considering higher education. Postsecondary DS providers, in collaboration with colleagues across campus in both Student and Academic Affairs, need to be proactive and creative in order to meet the needs of this emerging population. Other key players include, but are not limited to, external veteran affairs organizations, campus counseling and mental health centers, financial aid offices, and residential life and academic advising professionals.

Chronic Illness. Improvements in medical treatments have resulted in greater numbers of young adults with chronic illness pursuing postsecondary education (Barakat and Wodka 2006). While students with chronic health illnesses have similar needs to other students with disabilities, they also have unique and challenging issues that may require a deviation from the more standard accommodations. Due to their invisible nature, some illnesses may lead others to doubt a legitimate need for accommodations (Royster and Marshall 2008) and may require frequent absences from class during acute episodes or exacerbations. Students may then be reluctant to self-identify and request accommodations from faculty who may not see any obvious impairment. It is imperative for DS providers to foster supportive environments that inform faculty, in order to determine reasonable accommodations that do not compromise the academic integrity of the institution and to ensure appropriate treatment of students.

Student Athletes. Student athletes with disabilities can have a very different experience in college than athletes without disabilities. These students often try to perfect a balancing act between practice, games, classes, and homework. It is critical that more focus is placed on time management due to the increased complexity of college-level work, a busy athletic competition practice and game schedule, and how their disability affects them at the collegiate level (Stone 2005). Students must also comply with the National Collegiate Athletic Association (NCAA) eligibility requirements, which vary based on the institutional placement in Division I, II, or III. If students choose to engage in the NCAA process to have eligibility modifications made, they must identify their education-impacting disability and fill out specific forms. Depending on the institutional requirements for receiving accommodations, students may also be required to self-identify with the appropriate college or university official in order to receive academic accommodations (Walker 2005). The NCAA does not share the student's disability status with the institution (NCCA Regulations 2010–2011). While many student athletes have been diagnosed with learning disabilities (LDs) and attention deficit/hyperactivity disorder (ADD/ADHD), other disabilities including anxiety, depression, and other psychiatric disorders persist and are not widely talked about within this community (Walker 2005). Based on these complexities, collaborative efforts with athletic counselors are particularly important for DS to reassure student athlete concerns regarding self-identification to the disability service provider, out of fear of stigma from coaches and peers.

International Students. International students with disabilities have their own unique challenges in their transition to postsecondary environments. While their transition issues may be similar to other college-age students, they are also adjusting to a completely new culture. It is important to remember that the term *disability* and how people become "disabled" varies in every country (Reid and Knight 2006). Essentially, some students may have been considered nondisabled in their home country but disabled in the United States, or, quite possibly, the reverse. This can create confusion and challenges to adjustment and may adversely affect whether students self-identify to campus disability services providers. International students with disabilities who are more confident, more fluent in English, and have a sense of well-being often make a more successful transition to U.S. campuses (Hannigan 2000). With an increasing focus on globalization, it is critically important that international students are apprised of their rights and responsibilities under U.S. disability rights statutes, given that such legislation may not exist in their home country. DS professionals should also appropriately counsel students with disabilities who plan to study in other countries (Sygall and Lewis 2006). Proactive collaborative strategies and cross-training with study abroad offices and international student personnel is essential to ensure that students are fully apprised of the complexity of these issues.

Collaborative Programming Liaison System

The main goal of developing and cultivating liaisons across campus is to create relationships that foster opportunities to share and exchange information in an effort to meet the needs of students with disabilities more effectively and efficiently. At the CSD, each staff member serves as the liaison to specific departments across campus. Examples include but are not limited to: Admissions, Facilities and Engineering, Health Services, Registrars, Athletics, Dining Services, Study Abroad, and Career Services, as well as individual schools and colleges. Each liaison is charged with several responsibilities: (1) to share pertinent information as it relates to students with disabilities with each of their assigned departments; (2) to explore opportunities for collaborative programming for students with disabilities; (3) to provide technical assistance with regard to access concerns (whether physical or programmatic); and (4) to communicate information back to students in order to keep them apprised of opportunities for involvement. The liaison system has been extremely effective and, in fact, was adopted by other departments within Student Affairs at the University of Connecticut. By partnering with colleagues across campus, DS professionals can do their jobs more efficiently in order to meet the needs of this growing population of students, while assuring that colleagues from other functional areas understand the needs of students with disabilities and do not unwittingly discriminate against students.

External Outreach Initiatives

Students with disabilities often begin their college searches early, as it is important that the institution they choose is the right fit for them. These students will pay more attention to the special services and programs available at colleges and universities than their nondisabled peers (Korbel and Saunders 2008). It is vitally important that students are aware of the programs and services offered at a given institution, and that they understand the distinct differences between high school and college. Understanding the critical nature of this process, the CSD has several initiatives that facilitate this planning.

Secondary Personnel Day. This is a full-day collaborative program that invites secondary personnel to participate in an interactive and informative workshop to address the unique needs of students with disabilities transitioning to college. While the program resources are specific to the University of Connecticut, much of the information is transferrable to other settings. Connecticut's State Department of Education transition coordinator assists in the planning and assists with information dissemination. In addition to learning about the programs and services offered by the Center, there are also presentations by various campus departments, and a resource fair where attendees have an opportunity to address specific issues and concerns directly with campus representatives or DS personnel. Some of the offices represented include Financial Aid, Residential Life, and Admissions. Due in part to the ongoing collaborations between the Center and other departments at the University, this workshop is an exceptional medium to demonstrate the entire University's commitment to serving students with disabilities.

Survivor: College Edition. This informational workshop offers high school students and their family members a forum to learn about specific transition issues. Students participate in a college lecture and tour the campus. Two strands are provided—one for students and another for family members. Student participants learn about their rights and responsibilities under the Americans with Disabilities Act (ADA), the college application process, accommodations, learning strategies, and technologies, and participate in a college lecture.

Lunch and Learn. The CSD established the "Lunch and Learn" workshop series in an effort to reach out across functional areas of the Division of Student Affairs, promoting inclusion and encouraging conversations regarding students with disabilities. In addition, it is an exceptional opportunity to professionals to collaborate and share relevant information about working with students with disabilities. "Lunch and Learn" workshops are presented by CSD staff on various disability-related topics, such as the ADA and the recently passed Americans with Disabilities Act Amendments Act (ADAAA) and its implications for service delivery. Other topics include working with various types of students with disabilities, community standards, learning technologies, and other topics of interest to student affairs professionals. Presenting this information in a casual milieu allows colleagues to come together to share ideas, ask questions, and learn effective and useful strategies to bring back to their respective departments. On occasion, workshops are presented with professionals from other departments. The learning outcomes consistently focus on enhancing an inclusive environment and promoting success for students with disabilities. Likewise, this learning experience allows representatives from various student affairs offices to share information about policies, procedures, and events in their own departments with CSD staff. Exchanging knowledge in this manner is deliberate and comprehensive, and also ensures that staff will provide accurate information to students. The ability to offer students information about multiple departments in one setting affords students with more time for school work and extracurricular activities, ultimately leading to better student engagement (Whitt et al. 2008). For students with disabilities, feeling engaged in the campus community is vital for their development and success, perhaps more so than for other students (Nichols and Quaye 2009). It is with this knowledge that the CSD designed the "Lunch and Learn" model. These informal meetings have strengthened relationships within the division and enhanced opportunities for departments to join resources and create innovative programs for students. They also enhance the student experience and provide connectedness to the institution, which is critical for all students (see, e.g., Kuh 2009).

Summary

With an ever-changing higher education landscape for students with disabilities, it is increasingly important for student affairs practitioners to make certain that the campus community is not only prepared to accommodate these students and to ensure nondiscriminatory practices (Burke et al. 2010) but to also assist in the increasingly complex transition process. Collaboration will continue to be the cornerstone of accessible and inclusive transition strategies to promote student success.

References

American Council on Education (ACE). 2008. "Serving Those Who Serve: Higher Education and America's Veterans." Accessed March 1, 2010. http://www.acenet.edu /Content/NavigationMenu/ProgramsServices/MilitaryPMilitar/serving/Veterans_Issue _Brief_1108.pdf.

American Psychiatric Association. 2000. *Diagnostic and Statistical Manual of Mental Disorders: DSM-IV-TR*. Washington, DC: American Psychiatric Association.

Barakat, L. P., and E. L. Wodka. 2006. "Posttraumatic Stress Symptoms in College Students with a Chronic Illness." *Social Behavior and Personality* 34 (8): 999–1006.

Burke, L. A., J. Friedl, and M. Rigler. 2010. "The 2008 Ammendments to the Americans with Disabilities Act: Implications for Student Affairs Practitioners." *Journal of Student Affairs Research and Practice* 44 (4): 63–77.

Coll, J. E., H. Oh, C. Joyce, and L. C. Coll. 2009. "Veterans in Higher Education: What Every Adviser May Want to Know." *The Mentor: An Academic Advising Journal*, April 29. Accessed May 19, 2009. http://www.psu.edu/dus/mentor/090429jc.htm.

Dworkin, S. H. 2000. "Individual Therapy with Lesbian, Gay, and Bisexual Clients." In *Handbook of Counseling and Psychotherapy with Lesbian, Gay, and Bisexual Clients*, edited by R. M. Perez, K. A. DeBord, and K. J. Bieschke. Washington, DC: American Psychological Association.

Farmour-Dougan, V., D. James, and K. McKinney. 2000. "Student Engagement at Illinois State: Predictors of High Engagement." Unpublished paper. Normal: Center for Teaching, Learning and Technology, Illinois State University.

Hannigan, T. P. 2000. "Mental Health Issues of Students Who Cross Borders." *International Education* Summer: 18–23.

Harbour, W. S. 2008. *Final Report: The 2008 Biennial AHEAD Survey of Disability Services and Resource Professionals in Higher Education*. Huntersville, NC: Association on Higher Education And Disability (AHEAD).

Henry, W., K. Fuerth, and J. Figliozzi. 2010. "Gay with a Disability: A College Student's Multiple Cultural Journey." *College Student Journal* 44 (2): 377–88.

Korbel, D., and S. Saunders. 2008, June. "Doing More with Less: How to Work Smarter Not Harder by Collaborating with Colleagues." Presentation at the Postsecondary Disability Training Institute, Philadelphia.

Kuh, G. D. 2009. "What Student Affairs Professionals Need to Know about Student Engagement." *Journal of College Student Development* 50 (6): 683–706.

National Alliance on Mental Illness. 2009. "Depression Survey Initiative." Accessed August 3, 2010. http://www.nami.org/Content/NavigationMenu/Mental_Illnesses /Depression/NAMIDepressionReportFINAL.pdf.

National Center for Education Statistics (NCES). 2009. "Number and Percentage Distribution of Students Enrolled in Postsecondary Institutions, by Level, Disability Status, and Selected Student and Characteristics: 2003–04 and 2007–08." *Digest of Education Statistics.* Accessed July 20, 2010. http://nces.ed.gov/programs/digest/d09 /tables/dt09_231.asp.

National Collegiate Athletic Association (NCAA). 2010. *2010–2011 NCAA Division I Manual.* Indianapolis: NCAA.

National Institutes of Health. 2010. "Asperger Syndrome Fact Sheet." Accessed August 1, 2010. http://www.ninds.nih.gov/disorders/asperger/detail_asperger.htm.

Nichols, A. H., and S. J. Quaye. 2009. "Beyond Accommodation: Removing Barriers to Academic and Social Engagement for Students with Disabilities." In *Student Engagement in Higher Education: Theoretical Perspectives and Practical Approaches for Diverse Populations,* edited by S. R. Harper and S. J. Quaye. New York: Routledge.

Rand Center for Military Health Policy Research. 2008. "Invisible Wounds: Mental Health and Cognitive Care Needs of America's Returning Veterans." Accessed March 1, 2010. http://www.rand.org/pubs/research_briefs/2008/RAND_RB9336.pdf.

Reid, D. K., and M. G. Knight. 2006. "Disability Justifies Exclusion of Minority Students: A Critical History Grounded in Disability Studies." *Educational Researcher* 35: 18–23.

Royster, L., and O. Marshall. 2008. "The Chronic Illness Initiative: Supporting College Students with Chronic Illness Needs at DePaul University." *Journal of Postsecondary Education and Disability* 20 (2): 120–25.

Stone, D. H. 2005. "The Game of Pleasant Diversion: Can We Level the Playing Field for the Disabled Athlete and Maintain the National Pastime, in the Aftermath of *PGA Tour v. Martin*: An Empirical Study of the Disabled Athlete." *St. John's Law Review* 79: 377.

Sygall, S., and C. Lewis. 2006. *Building Bridges: A Manual on Including People with Disabilities in International Exchange Programs.* Eugene, OR: National Clearinghouse on Disability and Exchange, Mobility International USA.

Walker, Y. N. 2005. "Playing the Game of Academic Integrity vs. Athletic Success: The Americans with Disabilities Act (ADA) and Intercollegiate Student-Athletes with Learning Disabilities." *Marquette Sports Law Review* 15: 601.

Whitt, E. J., A. H. Kellogg, B. E. Nesheim, W. M. McDonald, M. J. Goentzel, and C. A. Wells. 2008. "Principles of Good Practice for Academic and Student Affairs Partnership Programs." *Journal of College Student Development* 49 (3): 235–49.

Wolf, L. E., J. Thierfeld-Brown, and R. G. Kukiela. 2009. *Students with Asperger's Syndrome: A Guide for College Personnel.* Shawnee Mission, KS: Autism Asperger Publishing Co.

DONNA M. KORBEL *is the Director of the Center for Students with Disabilities, Co-Director Center on Postsecondary Education and Disability, and a Higher Education and Student Affairs faculty member at the University of Connecticut.*

JENNIFER H. LUCIA *is the Associate Director of the Center for Students with Disabilities at the University of Connecticut, where she coordinates all new student referrals and residential accommodations.*

CHRISTINE M. WENZEL *is the Assistant Director of the Center for Students with Disabilities at the University of Connecticut, where she specializes in services and programming for students on the autism spectrum.*

BRYANNA G. ANDERSON *is a Disability Service Provider and Program Coordinator at the Center for Students with Disabilities at the University of Connecticut, where she coordinates study skills programs and secondary transition initiatives, including "Survivor: College Edition."*

NEW DIRECTIONS FOR HIGHER EDUCATION • DOI:10.1002/he

3

Reasonable accommodations are just one aspect of what disability services can offer campuses, and emerging ideas from the field may have implications for all students.

Disability Services Offices for Students with Disabilities: A Campus Resource

Rebecca C. Cory

What will campuses look like in ten years? In fifty? The swing toward using technology in teaching methodologies will no longer be cutting edge but will be commonplace. Students will be even more diverse than they are today, from various racial, social class, and geographic populations. The globalization of education will bring students from around the world to classes, possibly without moving physically. Students with more diverse disabilities will have supports to be fully included in K–12 general education classrooms, and therefore will be college eligible (Wagner et al. 2005; Wolanin and Steele 2004).

Section 504 of the 1973 Rehabilitation Act and the Americans with Disabilities Act (ADA) are often the starting places for conversations about students with disabilities in higher education. Section 504 and the ADA provide mandates for protection from discrimination and provision of reasonable disability accommodations (e.g., sign language interpreters, conversion of printed text to digital text, extended time on tests) (see Heyward, this volume). These laws guide work with students with disabilities on campus, but it is not enough. It is a good starting point, but should not be the ending point. Colleges and universities are committed to meeting more than the minimum legal obligations to students of color, women, and gay, lesbian, bisexual, and transgender (GLBT) students. Likewise, there should be a commitment to doing more than meeting a legal obligation for students with disabilities as well.

This chapter strives to help campus administrators understand obligations to students with disabilities, some current best practices in disability service provision, and timely issues challenging disability services (DS) staff in the United States. It frames disability services as both a legal and ethical obligation. There is an inherent tension in deciding how much to let the law

NEW DIRECTIONS FOR HIGHER EDUCATION, no. 154, Summer 2011 © Wiley Periodicals, Inc.
Published online in Wiley Online Library (wileyonlinelibrary.com) • DOI:10.1002/he.431

guide services, and how much to use DS resources to destigmatize disability and to create a campus that is inclusive and welcoming to all students.

Legal Compliance and DS Offices

Section 504 of the Rehabilitation Act of 1973 was the first law that pertained to access to higher education for students with disabilities, requiring colleges to provide disability accommodations and access, while protecting students from discrimination. This law was strengthened and broadened with the passage of the ADA in 1990 (and its reauthorization in 2008). The ADA mandates that places of public accommodation must provide protection from discrimination for and access to reasonable accommodations for otherwise qualified individuals with disabilities (see, e.g., Simon 2000).

There are a number of technical terms associated with these laws, with the three following terms being especially important for campus administrators and faculty to understand (for more information, see, e.g., Frank and Wade 1993; Madaus and Shaw 2004; Simon 2000; Wolanin and Steele 2004; see also Heyward, this volume).

Protection from Discrimination and "Essential Elements." Policies and procedures may not discriminate or seem to discriminate against people with disabilities, and must be flexible enough to not discriminate intentionally or unintentionally.

An example of unintentional discrimination would be an art class where students must stand at an easel while they draw or paint. The instructor may have good pedagogical reasons to have students stand and may believe that standing creates better art. Students may even prefer to stand. But this policy, on its face, rules out students with some types of disabilities, such as paraplegia, chronic fatigue, or balance issues. Masterpieces can and have been painted from seated or prone positions, so to implement and enforce this type of policy based on preference can seem discriminatory and therefore should be avoided.

Policies and procedures may, however, set technical standards for a degree program based on essential requirements for an academic or professional discipline. For example, a nursing program may require that a student have sufficient visual acuity to see changes in skin coloration of a patient. This is a requirement based in the core goals of a program and therefore is permitted, even if it rules out individuals with some types of disabilities.

The difference in these two examples is whether the policy or requirement is linked to the essential core learning objectives of the course or degree program. Policies that may discriminate must be justifiably linked to the essential elements of a class or program. If there is an accommodation that would mitigate a student's inability to meet a requirement, it must be considered.

Reasonable Accommodations. As one might guess from the term, reasonable accommodations are a judgment call. What *reasonable* means varies from class to class and person to person. What is reasonable for one student in a course may or may not be reasonable for another student in that same course, or for a student with the same disability in a different class. This is why accommodations are determined through a dialogue with students, DS staff, and instructors on a case-by-case basis.

An example will help elucidate how the determination of *reasonable* is contextually changeable. A student with a learning disability may request a calculator as an accommodation in classes. This may be a reasonable accommodation for the student when taking a chemistry class or a higher-level math class. However, for a student in a developmental math class where essential parts of the curriculum include learning and demonstrating concepts of calculation, the calculator may not be reasonable. Therefore, the DS provider and instructor must engage in a dialogue with the student to determine whether the calculator is reasonable. If it is not, then they must also determine other possible accommodations that can assist the student in meeting the essential elements of the class. In this example, other accommodations may include the use of a number line or three-dimensional manipulative (e.g., stacking cubes) to help the student with visualization of a concept and accuracy of calculation.

Unfortunately, faculty and staff are in a position of having to follow the mandates of law when they may or may not understand the nuances and complexities of it; past experiences or good intentions toward students with disabilities may not be enough (Doña and Edmister 2001; Jensen et al. 2004; Salzberg et al. 2002). The DS office on campus can support them in operationalizing mandates of Section 504 the ADA, as well as the commitment of the institution to students with disabilities. Instructors cannot be expected to know every detail about every type of disability, and DS staff cannot be expected to know every academic discipline on campus. Together, however, faculty and DS should be able to create a plan for students that is effective in meeting disability-related needs and the needs of specific academic disciplines.

The Accommodations Process

As seen in the previous examples, the accommodations process is part science and part art, but DS offices are responsible for guiding the institutional guarantee of reasonable accommodations from the ADA (Simon 2000; Wolanin and Steele 2004). By law, students are expected to request accommodations, so typically the accommodations process begins with them. To ask for accommodations, students have to disclose their disability, and the institution is permitted to require third-party documentation of that disability (Simon 2000; Wolanin and Steele 2004), which usually comes from a medical doctor, a psychologist or counselor, or a K–12 school psychologist or special education department. In each case, the documentation should provide a clear diagnosis and the functional impact of the disability on college-related activities like participating in classes, doing homework, taking tests, working with others, and so on (see, e.g., Brinckerhoff, McGuire, and Shaw 2002; Shaw, Madaus, and Dukes 2009).

When the student first discloses his or her disability to DS, professionals engage the student in a discussion of how the disability may have an impact on the student in a college environment. The conversation focuses on the classroom, the co-curricular environment, and, if the campus has housing, the living environment. DS staff can guide students in considering access to all aspects of the campus, in and out of the classroom (Strange, 2000).

Typically, DS staff will sit down with students to have these detailed conversations when the students decide to attend the college, at the beginning of their first semester, or as soon as the student discloses the disability to the institution (which may or may not be at the beginning of their time on campus) (Getzel 2005; Goode 2007; Shaw et al. 2009; Wolanin and Steele 2004). In this conversation, the DS staff member establishes a relationship with the student, learns about his or her academic goals and experiences, discusses any pertinent disability history and impact of the disability, and takes requests for accommodations. In this conversation, the DS staff will listen to what the student says and verify it with the third-party documentation of the disability. Using the documentation and the student's report, the staff member will make accommodation recommendations, which are usually presented to faculty in the form of a letter about accommodations. The letters are usually given to students, who deliver them to their instructors and teaching assistants personally. Ideally, students use the letters to initiate conversations about their needs.

Consultations with DS Offices

Another major role of the DS office is to work with faculty and staff to ensure the campus commitment to students with disabilities (Salzberg et al. 2002; Shaw and Dukes 2001). This is done through campus training and one-on-one meetings with instructors and staff. Administrators, faculty, and staff should see the DS office as a resource for all aspects of access: the larger picture of accessible curriculum design and universal design on campus, as well as the smaller picture of problem-solving situations with individual students or specific course components.

Many DS professionals are experts on accessible curriculum design, with a great wealth of knowledge on how to think through courses and points of access for students. Although DS staff members cannot be expected to know about all the academic disciplines offered on campus, they can work with instructors to create accessible or universally designed activities for students. DS may also be able to assist faculty in finding other state, local, or national resources for instructors.

DS staff are also always willing to consult with an instructor about the particular circumstances of a student in their class. If recommended accommodations are not appropriate or not working, instructors should arrange to meet with DS staff for a consultation. DS staff are there, in part, to take the administrative burden of accommodations off of instructors, including researching solutions to dilemmas and proposing alternatives to instructors. However, the professor is, as always, the ultimate authority on his or her courses and academic disciplines.

Current Issues in Provision of Disability Service

Alternative Media. With more and more students having print-related disabilities like dyslexia or visual impairments, as well as the increased use of electronic media and distance learning, access to educational material for students with disabilities is a hot topic (see, e.g., Edyburn, this volume). Technology has become both a path to access and a barrier to access for students with print-related disabilities like blindness, visual impairments, and print-based learning disabilities including dyslexia. Many students with print-related disabilities use computer software that enlarges text on the screen, reads the text aloud, types what the student is saying, or does some combination of these. Software packages such as Kurzweil and Jaws have given students increased access to electronic media. They can take an electronic document in Word, PDF, HTML, or other formats, and access the content independently. If these documents are formatted in the right way, they are seamless for users. Instructors should generally try to follow the standards set forth in Section 508 of the Rehabilitation Act for accessibility in the design of their electronic media (see the Section 508 website at http://www.section508.gov/ for more information).

However, electronic media without the proper formatting and markup can create additional barriers to students with print-related disabilities. Flash media and files of text that are saved as images can be entirely inaccessible. Faculty must be vigilant to ensure that their electronic resources are marked up in ways that increase access rather than limit it. DS staff and campus information technology (IT) personnel can assist with recommendations about accessibility of electronic resources and digital files.

Emergent Populations. Students with autism or Asperger's diagnoses are among the most recent groups of students to increase in number on U.S. campuses (Harbour 2008). This may be due to the increasing prevalence of autism spectrum disorders in the general population (Rice 2009). These students often can be highly successful academically but may struggle socially both in and out of the classroom (for first-person accounts of these issues, see Prince-Hughes 2002). Having Asperger's syndrome does not mean that students have below-average intelligence, so if they meet entrance criteria for degree programs, students with this label can (and should be expected to) perform at the same level as their peers.

Often, students identified as having Asperger's may need more direct communication than faculty are used to providing. For example, an instructor may be used to simply skipping over a student's raised hand if that student is dominating the conversation. A student with Asperger's may need the instructor to explicitly say that other people need to have a turn, but the larger conversation can continue after class. Students with Asperger's may also prefer a routine and have a difficult time coping with changes or surprises. These students typically love and excel in classes that follow a predictable pattern. Instructors can help students cope with change by being explicit about it. They can say, for example, "Typically, we start class with a full class discussion, but today we are going to try something different and start class in small groups instead." This acknowledgment of change in routine is a simple accommodation that can help a student to not get overly frustrated with an unpredictable class day.

There is also an increasing movement to create spaces for individuals with intellectual disabilities (historically identified as having "mental retardation") on campus as well (for more information, see Grigal and Hart 2009). With the most recent reauthorization of the Higher Education Act in 2008, the U.S. Department of Education is now offering grants and work study to students with intellectual disabilities who are participating in campus-based transition programs before they graduate from high school. Depending on the campus or campus program, students may audit for-credit courses, learn independent living skills on campus, or explore some combination of these, often with aides or nondisabled student peers offering support (Grigal and Hart 2009). While many open-enrollment community colleges have had students with intellectual disabilities for decades, this movement remains controversial, as many professionals argue that this emerging population of students will compromise academic standards. However, initial research suggests that inclusion of students with significant disabilities can often exceed expectations of faculty and staff, do not demand any significant modification of course material for nondisabled students, and can contribute toward a positive classroom experience for everyone involved (see, e.g., Causton-Theoharis, Asby, and DeClouette 2009). Providing higher education opportunities to all people is a logical step toward a society committed to the inclusion of all people.

As was true at many times in the history of the United States, when we are at war or have just concluded a war, the access to education for returning veterans improves. With new GI Bills allowing more veterans to enter education, we are seeing this population increase on our campuses (Madaus, Miller, and Vance 2009). Many of these returning soldiers have physical and mental combat-related disabilities. The military culture teaches these students to be self-reliant and work hard, which can make them excellent students. However, they may have difficulty admitting the need for assistance—especially students who have psychiatric disabilities (Burnett and Segoria 2009; Madaus et al. 2009). However, the incidence of posttraumatic stress disorder (PTSD) is estimated to be as high as 20 percent in the returning veteran population (Roehr 2007). Students experiencing PTSD may have high absenteeism from classes or difficulty focusing and staying on task. These students are used to being tough under pressure and getting the job done. They can be frustrated by the civilian world and how it operates as well as frustrated by the new limitations of their body and mind. With appropriate supports—physical, social, and psychological—however, most are able to be successful students.

Universal Design. One solution for including all students with disabilities in a way that reduces stigma and the need for accommodation is to implement universal design (UD). UD is the design of environments, whether they be physical or curricular, to be accessible to the greatest diversity of individuals as possible. UD is a process of imagining the greatest diversity of your student body, with regard to race, class, gender, sexual orientation or identity, religion, ability, and age—and designing for that, rather than the historic practice of designing for a "typical" or "average" student and then making adjustments for every student who is "different" (Bowe 2000; Burgstahler and Cory 2008; McGuire, Scott, and Shaw 2004; Rose and Meyer 2002). UD creates an inclusive environment for all students and reduces the need for accommodations or specialized circumstances.

One of the shifts with UD is in how one thinks about accommodations. For example, in the past, a sign language interpreter was seen as an accommodation for a student who is deaf. Universal design does not do away with the need for interpreters, but it does change thinking about them. The "problem" shifts from the deaf student to the entire class. The class of nonsigning, nondeaf students has a communication problem with some people; class members communicate through sign or speech. Seeing the situation this way creates the need for an interpreter to facilitate *everyone's* communication. So the interpreter is there for the instructor, the deaf student, and the hearing students. Likewise, some disability accommodations, like class notes or choices about assignments (e.g., doing a presentation or a paper), may support all students' learning, encouraging creative and inclusive pedagogy while removing the stigma of accommodations as "special" considerations (Ben-Moshe et al. 2005; Rose et al. 2006).

Thinking of Disability as Part of Campus Diversity. Campus conversations about diversity are starting to include disability. With disability studies programs increasing on campuses, and the disability rights movement having a history and politics that are increasingly well known through mainstream books and media (e.g., Shapiro 1994), campuses are moving to embrace disability as diversity. Seeing disability as diversity is easier if disability is situated in culture and context rather than the person who has a disability (Linton 1998; Taylor, this volume). Then the problem, for example, is not that a person using a wheelchair cannot walk, but rather that designers of a campus space failed to put in adequate ramps and elevators. The solution is no longer focused on an individual but is systemic. This is a similar evolution to the shift in pathological thinking about race and gender over the years.

When campuses include disability in their conversations about diversity, they start to see that including individuals with disabilities as students, faculty and staff enhances the campus. This leads to creating a more inclusive environment.

Conclusion

Section 504 and the Americans with Disabilities Act give a framework for starting to discuss services for college students with disabilities. Institutions have the opportunity to challenge themselves to push past legal compliance to a place of inclusion and integration of students. With proper staffing of DS offices in support of students, newly emergent populations can thrive as well, and campuses can start to explore how disability can be celebrated as a part of campus diversity that ultimately fosters access for all students.

References

Ben-Moshe, L., R. C. Cory, M. Feldbaum, and K. Sagendorf, eds. 2005. *Building Pedagogical Curb Cuts: Incorporating Disability in the University Classroom and Curriculum.* Syracuse, NY: Graduate School Press, Syracuse University.

Bowe, F. G. 2000. *Universal Design in Education: Teaching Nontraditional Students.* Westport, CT: Bergin and Garvey.

Brinckerhoff, L. C., J. M. McGuire, and S. F. Shaw. 2002. *Postsecondary Education and Transition for Students with Learning Disabilities,* 2nd ed. Austin, TX: PRO-ED, Inc.

Burgstahler, S. E., and R. C. Cory, eds. 2008. *Universal Design in Higher Education: From Principles to Practice.* Cambridge, MA: Harvard Education Press.

Burnett, S. E., and J. Segoria. 2009. "Collaboration for Military Transition Students from Combat to College: It Takes a Community." *Journal of Postsecondary Education and Disability* 22 (1): 53–58.

Causton-Theoharis, J., C. Ashby, and N. DeClouette. 2009. "Relentless Optimism: Inclusive Postsecondary Opportunities for Students with Significant Disabilities." *Journal of Postsecondary Education and Disability* 22 (2): 88–105.

Doña, J., and J. H. Edmister. 2001. "An Examination of Community College Faculty Members' Knowledge of the ADA of 1990 at the Fifteen Community Colleges in Mississippi." *Journal of Postsecondary Education and Disability* 14 (2): 91–103.

Frank, K., and P. Wade. 1993. "Disabled Student Services in Postsecondary Education: Who's Responsible for What?" *Journal of College Student Development* 34: 26–30.

Getzel, E. E. 2005. "Preparing for College." In *Going to College: Expanding Opportunities for People with Disabilities,* edited by E. E. Getzel and P. Wehman. Baltimore: Paul H. Brookes.

Goode, J. 2007. "'Managing' Disability: Early Experiences of University Students with Disabilities." *Disability and Society* 22 (1): 35–48.

Grigal, M., and D. Hart. 2009. *Think College! Postsecondary Education Options for Students with Intellectual Disabilities.* Baltimore: Paul H. Brookes.

Harbour, W. S. 2008. *Final Report: The 2008 Biennial AHEAD Survey of Disability Services and Resource Professionals in Higher Education.* Huntersville, NC: Association on Higher Education And Disability (AHEAD).

Jensen, J. M., N. McCrary, K. Krampe, and J. Cooper. 2004. "Trying to Do the Right Thing: Faculty Attitudes toward Accommodating Students with Learning Disabilities." *Journal of Postsecondary Education and Disability* 17 (2): 81–90.

Linton, S. 1998. *Claiming Disability: Knowledge and Identity.* New York: New York University Press.

Madaus, J. W., W. K. Miller, and M. L. Vance. 2009. "Veterans with Disabilities in Postsecondary Education." *Journal of Postsecondary Education and Disability* 22 (1): 10–17.

Madaus, J. W., and S. F. Shaw. 2004. "Section 504: Differences in the Regulations for Secondary and Postsecondary Education." *Intervention in School and Clinic* 40 (2): 81–87.

McGuire, J. M., S. S. Scott, and S. F. Shaw. 2004. "Universal Design for Instruction: The Paradigm, Its Principles, and Products for Enhancing Instructional Access." *Journal of Postsecondary Education and Disability* 17 (1): 10–20.

Prince-Hughes, D., ed. 2002. *Aquamarine Blue 5.* Athens: Ohio University Press, 2002.

Rice, C. 2009. "Prevalence of Autism Spectrum Disorders—Autism and Developmental Disabilities Monitoring Network, United States, 2006." Centers for Disease Control and Prevention. Accessed December 31, 2010. http://www.cdc.gov/mmwr/preview/mmwrhtml/ss5810a1.htm.

Roehr, B. 2007."High Rate of PTSD in Returning Iraq War Veterans." *Medscape Medical News.* Accessed December 31, 2010. http://www.medscape.com/viewarticle/565407.

Rose, D. H., W. S. Harbour, C. S. Johnston, S. G. Daley, and L. Abarbanell, 2006. "Universal Design for Learning in Postsecondary Education: Reflections on Principles and Their Applications." *Journal of Postsecondary Education and Disability* 19 (2): 135–51.

Rose, D. H., and A. Meyer. 2002. *Teaching Every Student in the Digital Age: Universal Design for Learning.* Baltimore: Association for Supervision and Curriculum Development.

Salzberg, C. L., L. Peterson, C. C. Debrand, R. J. Blair, A. Carsey, and A. S. Johnson. 2002. "Opinions of Disability Service Directors on Faculty Training: The Need, Content, Issues, Formats, Media, and Activities." *Journal of Postsecondary Education and Disability* 15 (2): 101–14.

Shapiro, J. 1994. *No Pity: People with Disabilities Forging a New Civil Rights Movement.* New York: Crown Publishing Group.

Shaw, S. F., and L. L. Dukes. 2001. "Program Standards for Disability Services in Higher Education." *Journal of Postsecondary Education and Disability* 14 (2): 81–90.

Shaw, S. F., J. W. Madaus, and L. L. Dukes. 2009. *Preparing Students with Disabilities for College Success: A Practical Guide to Transition Planning.* Baltimore: Paul H. Brookes.

Simon, J. 2000. "Legal Issues in Serving Students with Disabilities in Postsecondary Education." In *Serving Students with Disabilities,* edited by H. A. Belch. New Directions for Student Services, no. 91. San Francisco: Jossey-Bass.

Strange, C. 2000. "Creating Environments of Ability." In *Serving Students with Disabilities,* edited by H. A. Belch. New Directions for Student Services, no. 91. San Francisco: Jossey-Bass.

Wagner, M., L. Newman, R. Cameto, and P. Levine. 2005. *Changes Over Time in the Early Postschool Outcomes of Youth with Disabilities: A Report of Findings from the National Longitudinal Transition Study (NLTS) and the National Longitudinal Transition Study-2 (NLTS2).* Menlo Park, CA: SRI International.

Wolanin, T. R., and P. E. Steele. 2004. *Higher Education Opportunities for Students with Disabilities: A Primer for Policymakers.* Washington, DC: Institute for Higher Education Policy.

REBECCA C. CORY *is the Manager of Disability Services at North Seattle Community College. She is coeditor of* Building Pedagogical Curbcuts: Incorporating Disability in the University Classroom *(Syracuse University Press, 2005) and* Universal Design in Higher Education: From Principles to Practice *(Harvard Education Press, 2008).*

NEW DIRECTIONS FOR HIGHER EDUCATION • DOI:10.1002/he

4

Campuses can use technology to implement universal design in instruction and learning, with benefits for all students.

Harnessing the Potential of Technology to Support the Academic Success of Diverse Students

Dave Edyburn

Higher education administrators are well aware of the time, energy, and resources devoted to programs on their campus that have been designed to enhance the retention and success of diverse students. Similarly, administrators recognize the rapid rate of change in the technology marketplace and the significant costs associated with acquiring, implementing, and maintaining educational technologies required to keep a college or university up to date. However, unless technology is a personal passion of the higher education administrator, it is difficult to properly evaluate the latest widget from new tools that have significant potential for enhancing academic success. Seldom do we examine the nexus of technology and its potential role for fostering academic success for students in the bottom 50th percentile.

The purpose of this chapter is to introduce administrators to the principles of universal design (UD) for learning. The goal is to explain how UD principles can be implemented using technology, in ways that will explicitly target the special needs of learners with disabilities, but will offer educational benefit to all students. The value of this approach is that busy administrators will be able to articulate a clear philosophy regarding the alignment of technology in postsecondary education and improved student outcomes; "check point" questions at the end of each subsection can further assist in clarifying individual and campus philosophies. On a practical level, readers will learn about resources, strategies, and tools that will support faculty and students in building academic success.

NEW DIRECTIONS FOR HIGHER EDUCATION, no. 154, Summer 2011 © Wiley Periodicals, Inc.
Published online in Wiley Online Library (wileyonlinelibrary.com) • DOI:10.1002/he.432

Recognizing Academic Diversity

American classrooms at every level of education are more diverse than ever before (Gebeloff, Evans, and Scheinkman 2010). However, few teachers and professors are adequately prepared to effectively teach diverse learners. As a result, we tend to play "Mirror, Mirror on the Wall—Who Is the Best Teacher of Them All?" Rather than look at all of our students, we tend to think about our best students and walk away from the mirror with great satisfaction. Since our teaching prowess was just verified, we believe that the chronic underachievement of students in the bottom 50th percentile is not our problem. Those students should be required to take remedial classes, go to the tutoring center, visit the writing center, or be referred to the disability student services office. After all, we are great teachers.

Unless professors and administrators understand that academic diversity is a characteristic, not a flaw, of every classroom, campuses will continue to devote significant resources to providing remedial support services and individual disability accommodations. Arguably, current student support services are not effective when we see poor retention rates, high dropout rates, low graduation rates, and excessive time for degree completion within subgroups of diverse students (e.g., students of color and students with disabilities) (Hurst and Smerdon 2000; U.S. Government Accountability Office 2009). Undoubtedly, the student success initiatives currently being implemented on campuses are explicitly designed to address one or more of the statistics associated with academic failure.

Efforts to enhance the success of twenty-first-century learners will require a fundamental shift in thinking about, and responding to, learner differences. Rose and Meyer (2002) argue that we should not think about students as being disabled, but rather consider the curriculum disabled, as it poses barriers to access, engagement, and success. Tomlinson (2004) recommends thinking about learning differences as a Mobius strip: a continuum of knowledge and skills with no clear demarcation on the journey from the starting point as novice and the end point as expert. McLeskey and Waldon (2007) suggest that classrooms must be places where differences are ordinary. In most classrooms, the acceptable range of learner variance is very narrow, and differences outside of this band are considered problems for someone else to deal with.

Checkpoint. Is academic diversity a condition to be remediated or celebrated? When students struggle in a course, what does this signify? To what extent should every class be explicitly designed to support students with diverse interests, background knowledge, and skills?

Responding to Academic Diversity by Proactively Valuing Differences

If we begin with the premise that every classroom is composed of diverse learners, we start from a different point than traditional instruction, where

**Figure 4.1. Screen Print of the Website "The Brain"
(at http://thebrain.mcgill.ca).**

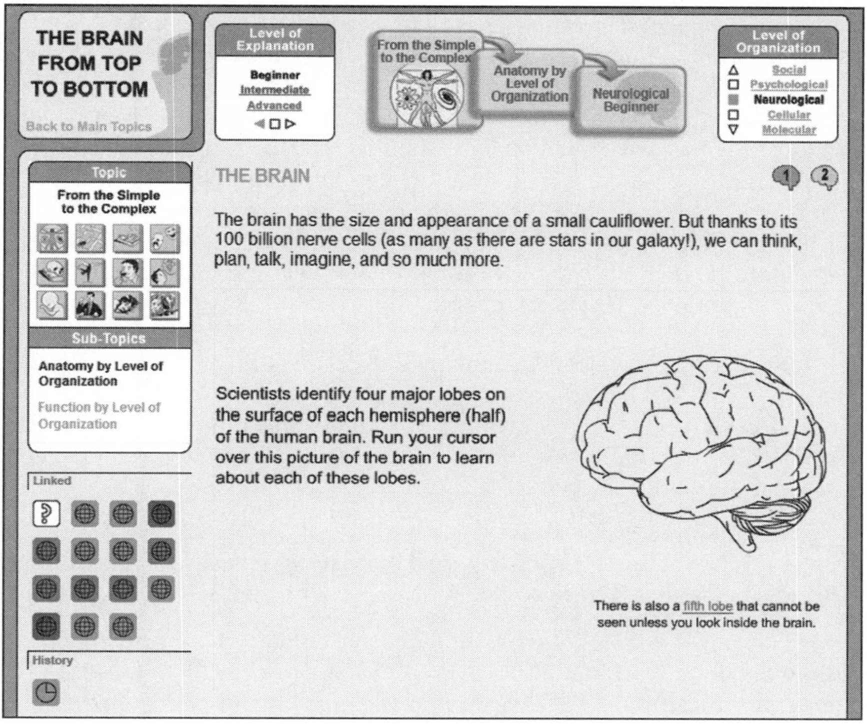

content is the exclusive focus. Rather, we begin to think about how we can support diverse learners before they have a chance to fail. This mind-set establishes the need for technology, since digital media offers flexibility and tools not available with traditional instructional tools of chalkboards, textbooks, paper, and pencils. Indeed, technology is essential for supporting the academic success of diverse learners.

In a traditional classroom that relies primarily on a printed textbook, diverse students may encounter a variety of problems in accessing and understanding the information. In this case, they must seek out campus support services. However, when the instructional needs of diverse students are considered as a curricular design principle, course content can be created in a digital environment, with a wide variety of supports built in that can be used by all learners. Advances in technology afford new opportunities to abandon the mistaken assumption about curriculum design that one size fits all.

Consider the example of a page from the website "The Brain," as shown in Figure 4.1. This web page contains basic facts about the brain and its anatomy, with a simple line drawing of a brain. The same information could

NEW DIRECTIONS FOR HIGHER EDUCATION • DOI:10.1002/he

be presented in a textbook. However, fixed print could pose a barrier for students who are blind or have low vision because they may have difficulty in reading the text. With digital text, all learners can read and manipulate the text to enhance learning. Any student can use browser controls (e.g., view, zoom in/out) to adjust the size of the text and images on a web page. If students are unable to read a section of text, they can highlight the text, copy it, and then paste it into a web-based text-to-speech program like Vozme (http://www.vozme.com) to listen to information they cannot read independently. Because this site was created at McGill University, where a majority of students speak French, the entire site is available in both English and French. In addition, the site uses a design principle known as *tiering*, where the text is available at three levels (beginner, intermediate, and expert) to allow students to access the information that is appropriate for their understanding.

Checkpoint. If we truly understand diversity and value learner differences, what should be different about the classroom and instruction, before the students arrive? How can we use our knowledge of student differences and instructional challenges to design learning environments and materials in ways that provide support to all students before anyone fails?

New Insights About Teaching and Learning from Universal Design Theory

Recent advances in cognitive psychology have enhanced our understanding of how the brain works (Bransford, Brown, and Cocking 2000; Jensen 2009; van Gog et al. 2005) and have important implications for the design of twenty-first-century learning materials and environments. These advances have informed the development of a philosophy about universal design for learning. Universal design for learning proactively values learner differences by embedding supports required by some students into learning materials and environments, so all students can use them as needed (Pisha and Coyne 2001; Rose and Meyer 2002; Scott, McGuire, and Shaw 2003). Educators who use this philosophy seek to move beyond the one-size-fits-all paradigm, considering how to provide instruction that allows for three principles of universal design for learning (UDL): multiple means of representing curricular information (e.g., text, video, audio, multimedia), multiple means of expressing what one has learned, and multiple means of engaging in the learning tasks (Rose and Meyer 2002).

One of the key tools for implementing a universal design for learning philosophy involves recognizing the value of digital media. Digital media offers flexibility that is not found in print. Whereas printed text is fixed (size, color, spacing), the physical appearance of digital text can be altered by the user, converted from text to audio, and translated from one language to another. Other supports (e.g., definitions, hints, how-to guides) and scaffolds (i.e., avatar coaches) can also be embedded in digital text to support diverse learners. As a result, technology is deemed to be essential in supporting UDL (Edyburn 2010).

One of the primary factors contributing to technology's application of the UDL principle of engagement involves the interactive nature of technology. Completing math problems on the computer, with feedback, is far superior to completing the same problems on paper, turning the assignment in to the professor, and waiting two to five days for feedback on one's performance. Additionally, interactive digital learning materials provide significant opportunities for choice, personalization, and just-in-time support. The research on the development of expertise is very clear: repeated engagement, over time, with tasks of increasing difficulty, is the recipe for fostering high levels of expertise (Bransford, Brown, and Cocking 2000; Hattie 2009). UDL offers a framework for engaging diverse learners in deeper and more meaningful learning.

Campuses are encouraged to develop diversity blueprints or campus diversity assessments. That is, how do we understand the important ways that students are different (e.g., background knowledge, writing skills)? Thinking about each of these factors as a continuum provides a mechanism for differentiating and planning supports. Then, how can this blueprint be used to develop universal design strategies that ensure that these differences are valued and supported? Aligning technology initiatives with the diversity blueprint will be a significant step toward investing in academic success.

Checkpoint. Educators and administrators frequently make assumptions that all learners learn like they do. As a result, we are often surprised when students struggle to be successful in the classroom. How can we facilitate discussions about recent advances in the learning sciences, to create instructional environments and materials that proactively value academic diversity and engage students in developing high levels of expertise? How can we help faculty move away from goals of covering the curriculum and toward goals of teaching for understanding?

Applications of Technology

Surveys of technology trends in higher education routinely identify the ever-shifting focus on what is new (Johnson, Levine, and Smith 2009). Higher education administrators frequently receive proposals about the need to acquire the latest technologies (e.g., iPads, e-book readers, cloud computing, digital whiteboards, 1-1 laptop initiatives). However, these proposals are usually based on the needs of early adopters to have the latest technologies. Administrators should challenge the early adopters who advance these proposals to explicitly define how diverse students, including students with disabilities, will benefit from these technological innovations. We must be cautious when adopting technologies without a clear understanding of their value for learning. Unfortunately, purchasing more digital whiteboards is not likely to have the same impact as purchasing netbooks. Therefore,

New Directions for Higher Education • DOI:10.1002/he

administrators are advised to encourage initiatives on the learning side of the teaching and learning equation.

When faculty members provide readings in multiple formats (e.g., print, PDF, HTML), we see evidence of enhanced access to the curriculum. When students are taught to use the AutoSummary feature in Microsoft Word to create summaries of challenging readings, we see evidence of enhanced engagement and outcomes as a result of their efforts to alter the challenge level. When faculty members use tic-tac-toe grids to provide their students with choices for completing a learning assignment, we see evidence of enhanced engagement. When faculty members make assignments that require collaborative writing using Google Docs (http://docs.google.com) or Zoho Writer (http://writer.zoho.com/), we are able to collect local evidence of enhanced engagement and outcome.

Checkpoint. Many campus administrators are responsible for approving technology requests that are prepared simply to remain cutting edge. Such initiatives will facilitate change in the academic performance of diverse students. In what ways can administrators use the acquisition of technology as a core strategy for supporting the academic success of diverse students? Given a choice between investments in technology that enhances teaching, and investments in technology that enhances learning, preference must be given to the latter.

Leadership and Action Planning

Few postsecondary institutions have a vision for deploying technology in ways that work toward reducing achievement gaps. As a result, higher education administrators are encouraged to consider top-down, bottom-up, and policy change strategies that align technology with institutional initiatives for enhancing the academic success of diverse learners.

Top-down change strategies are necessary in defining the mission and core values of learning organizations (Senge et al. 2000). Therefore, attention should also be devoted to technology supports that are provided outside of the classroom. For example, web-based forms such as Ask a Librarian allow students to seek help whenever and wherever they need it. Likewise, online writing labs (OWLs) can offer resources, guidance, and support for students as they write class papers. Students who need specialized technology tools, like scan-and-read systems, should be able to access free assistive technology (see, e.g., http://www.rsc-ne-scotland.ac.uk/eduapps/help.php) through campus technology services (Houchins 2001). As many campuses expand their online course offerings, they are recognizing the need to consolidate and improve the profile of online campus support services.

Administrators must also create a culture that facilitates bottom-up change. That is, how will faculty and staff have the resources to enhance the success of diverse learners? Workshops on universal design for learning will facilitate this conversation and subsequent skill development (Izzo, Murray, and Novak 2008). Course improvement minigrants will provide faculty with the incentive and time to learn news tools and integrate UD for learning strategies in their courses. In addition, faculty should be challenged to use basic research designs (e.g., pre-post, single subject) to collect evidence about how the instructional innovations affect student learning.

An important tool for higher education administrators is policy change. When institutional policies prevent faculty from installing software on a campus computer, or locked ports prevent students from using accessibility software on their USB drives, it is clear that the institution is confused about whether security is more important than student learning. The policy message must be clear: all campus technology efforts must focus on fostering higher levels of student learning.

Checkpoint. What does a higher education administrator need to know and do, relative to using technology, to support diverse students? One critical action is to advocate for the alignment of technology and improved student outcomes. Universal design for learning provides a framework for proactively valuing academic diversity by explicitly targeting the special needs of diverse learners, while offering educational benefit to all students. Finally, administrators need to employ top-down change strategies, facilitate bottom-up change strategies, and utilize policy change as a means of making differences ordinary.

Summary

Whereas campus administrators are faced with relentless demands to acquire new technologies as a means of keeping up with all that the marketplace has to offer, it is necessary to align technology acquisition with institutional goals and activities for enhancing retention, reducing time to degree completion, and raising graduation rates. Universal design for learning (UDL) offers theory and practice principles for designing learning environments and materials where supports are embedded to support learning for all students. Administrators are encouraged to use top-down, bottom-up, and policy change strategies to utilize the latest advances in the learning sciences to inform the acquisition and deployment of technologies. Such efforts must be considered strategic investments in the success of all students.

References

Bransford, J. D., A. L. Brown, and R. R. Cocking. 2000. *How People Learn: Brain, Mind, Experience, and School.* Washington, DC: National Academies Press, 2000.

Edyburn, D. L. 2010. "Would You Recognize Universal Design for Learning if You Saw It? Ten Propositions for New Directions for the Second Decade of UDL." *Learning Disability Quarterly* 33 (1): 33–41.

Gebeloff, R., T. Evans, and A. Scheinkman. 2010. "Diversity in the Classroom." Accessed November 23, 2010. http://projects.nytimes.com/immigration/enrollment.

Hattie, J. A. 2009. *Visible Learning: A Synthesis of Over 800 Meta-Analyses Relating to Achievement.* New York: Routledge.

Houchins, D. E. 2001. "Assistive Technology Barriers and Facilitators during Secondary and Post-Secondary Transitions." *Career Development for Exceptional Individuals* 24: 73–88.

Hurst, D., and B. Smerdon. 2000. *Postsecondary Students with Disabilities: Enrollment, Services, and Persistence.* Washington, DC: National Center for Education Statistics.

Izzo, M. V., A. Murray, and J. Novak. 2008. "The Faculty Perspective on Universal Design for Learning." *Journal of Postsecondary Education and Disability* 21 (2): 60–72.

Jensen, E. 2009. *Teaching with Poverty in Mind: What Being Poor Does to Kids' Brains and What Schools Can Do About It.* Thousand Oaks, CA: Corwin Press.

Johnson, L., A. Levine, and R. Smith. 2009. *The 2009 Horizon Report.* Austin, TX: New Media Consortium.

McLeskey, J., and N. Waldon. 2007. "Making Differences Ordinary in Inclusive Classrooms." *Intervention in School and Clinic* 42 (3): 162–68.

Pisha, B., and P. Coyne. 2001. "Smart from the Start: The Promise of Universal Design for Learning." *Remedial and Special Education* 22: 197–203.

Rose, D., and A. Meyer. 2002. *Teaching Every Student in the Digital Age.* Alexandria, VA: ASCD.

Scott, S. S., J. M. McGuire, and S. F. Shaw. 2003. "Universal Design for Instruction: A New Paradigm for Adult Instruction in Postsecondary Education." *Remedial and Special Education* 24 (6): 369–79.

Senge, P., N. Cambron-McCabe, T. Lucas, B. Smith, J. Dutton, and A. Kleiner. 2000. *Schools that Learn: A Fifth Discipline Fieldbook for Educators, Parents, and Everyone Who Cares about Education.* New York: Doubleday.

Tomlinson, C. A. 2004. "The Mobius Effect: Addressing Learner Variance in Schools." *Journal of Learning Disabilities* 37 (6): 516–24.

U.S. Government Accountability Office. 2009. *Higher Education and Disability: Education Needs a Coordinated Approach to Improve Its Assistance to Schools in Supporting Students.* Washington, DC: U.S. Government Accountability Office.

van Gog, T., K. A. Ericsson, P. M. Rikers, and F. Paas. 2005. "Instructional Design for Advanced Learners: Establishing Connections Between the Theoretical Frameworks of Cognitive Load and Deliberate Practice." *Educational Technology Research and Development* 53 (3): 73–81.

DAVE EDYBURN *is a professor in the University of Wisconsin–Milwaukee's Department of Exceptional Education, a member of the Advisory Board for the National Center on Universal Design for Learning, and coprincipal investigator of the federally funded Universal Design Infusion of Technology and Evaluation for Accessible Campuses of Higher Education (UDITEACH) Project.*

5

While the majority of disability services offices focus on students, the University of Minnesota has a unique model that also serves faculty and staff with disabilities and chronic conditions.

UReturn: University of Minnesota Services for Faculty and Staff with Disabilities

Dave Fuecker, Wendy S. Harbour

Healthy faculty and staff are essential for campuses to be competitive, yet the needs of faculty and staff with disabilities are still secondary for many campuses that have well-established services for students. No exact figures are available because higher education does not systematically collect information about employees' disabilities and because disability status may change over an employee's career. Some estimate that up to one in five faculty and staff in higher education have a disability or chronic health condition that may require accommodations or services at some time (Rothstein 2004). In businesses, human resources typically handles disability-related services (see, e.g., Nafukho, Roessler, and Kacirek 2010), but in higher education, many units may serve campus employees with disabilities: the Americans with Disabilities Act (ADA) and Section 504 Coordinator, Human Resources, Employee Benefits, or the Equal Opportunity and Affirmative Action office. On some campuses, different types of disability-related issues are handled by different departments, or accommodations and services are negotiated with direct supervisors (e.g., deans or department chairs) who may have no knowledge or experience related to disability. On 75 percent of campuses in the United States, the disability services office only serves students (Harbour 2004), and at the 2010 international conference for the Association on Higher Education And Disability (AHEAD) (the major professional organization for disability services providers), there were 126 concurrent sessions, but none of them explicitly focused on employees with disabilities (AHEAD 2010).

NEW DIRECTIONS FOR HIGHER EDUCATION, no. 154, Summer 2011 © Wiley Periodicals, Inc.
Published online in Wiley Online Library (wileyonlinelibrary.com) • DOI:10.1002/he.433

Yet there can be real advantages to having disability services offices address both student and employee concerns. The purpose of this chapter is to explain how Disability Services (DS) at the University of Minnesota–Twin Cities (UMN) began offering accommodations and services for employees, its strategies for providing services using a combination of centralized and decentralized approaches, and current issues facing the field. Recommendations are included for campuses that are just starting to serve employees in any systematic way.

Establishing Employee Services at the University of Minnesota

Until the early 1990s, UMN staff and faculty with disabilities were served by the Office of Human Resources (HR). HR was considered a "management consultant" for administrators, especially given the university's highly unionized environment. Administrators realized that employees were reluctant to provide administrators, including HR, with protected health information about disabilities, to let HR speak with medical providers, or to request necessary accommodations that may involve costs. While these are widespread problems among all employers (Baldridge and Veiga 2006), UMN was experiencing it firsthand. It was especially difficult for employees experiencing the onset of new health conditions, who may be unaware of their rights, worried about stigma associated with a health condition, or unclear about what they needed to continue working. Under federal laws, including the Americans with Disabilities Act (ADA) and Section 504 of the 1973 Rehabilitation Act, employees are not under any obligation to self-disclose their disability—so many employees were "slipping through the cracks." UMN general counsel and the campus ADA Coordinator (who was also director of the Equal Opportunity and Affirmative Action office) realized that employees needed to *perceive* disability services providers as being neutral, but ideally those staff would actually *be* neutral, as well.

In consultation with disability services, general counsel advised UMN to move employee services to Disability Services, partly to minimize legal risk. Initially, the Employee Services unit at DS was charged with accommodating nonoccupational injuries and illnesses in faculty and staff (i.e., not workers' compensation). The focus was protecting rights under disability laws, including the ADA and Title I. It quickly became evident, however, that determining who had a "disability" could be an all-consuming legal question, when even courts are still evolving in deciding who is "disabled" or not (Rothstein 2004). Employee Services quickly shifted from a focus on defining who had a disability to concerns about what is reasonable for a particular employee and job.

As an example, suppose an employee has a diagnosis of bipolar disorder that is treated with medication, and there is no real impact on his or her work (i.e., no functional limitations). This employee may or may not be covered under disability law (Americans with Disabilities Act Amendments Act [ADAAA]), and there are no accommodations necessary. But focusing on "what is reasonable" means being open to making occasional small adjustments or accommodations that may be needed. For instance, medication may cause the employee to be slow in the mornings and have a "hung-over" feeling. In that case, it may be reasonable to shift work hours from a 7:45 start to a 9:00 start, working a full eight hours from there. UMN leaders agreed that determining whether the person has a disability or is covered under the law is not so important as the question of how to reasonably support a person's continued employment.

The reason for this philosophical shift is largely to protect human capital; the university wants an employee to remain productive. Focusing on reasonable accommodations or services emphasizes productivity and work retention. Employees also have an identity at work: what they do, whom they work for, and why they like their job. A work-related identity is important to individuals, and those individuals are important to the institution. When a person's work identity is compromised because of a medical condition or disability, especially if it has a late onset (after hiring) or is exacerbated for any reason, then the identity as an employee is compromised. The longer it's compromised, the less likely an employee will return to work/return to that identity.

The name of Employee Services was changed to UReturn in 2005 to reflect their integrated approach to return-to-work/work retention, but the three cornerstones of Employee Services have remained the same since it moved from HR to DS: neutrality, confidentiality, and early intervention. Focusing on interpersonal reasons for accommodations, such as the benefits to one's self-worth or identity, helps retain employees and is in line with DS's progressive approaches to serving students. But at the same time, it's also cost-effective and minimizes legal risk. The shift from asking "Who is covered under the law?" to "What is reasonable for this individual?" is good business on many levels. Since moving from HR, the number of employees using UReturn has increased each year (at one point increasing 100 percent during a single academic year). Relationships with unions have also improved, with unions now considering DS a friend of unions and unionized employees with disabilities.

The Organization of DS and UReturn

The physical layout of Disability Services is a large inverted "U" shape (see Figure 5.1), with separate entrances for students and employees. Once inside, Student Services and UReturn both have receptionists and a waiting area. This physical separation of space was designed to encourage more use and privacy (so students and professors would be less likely to see each other while visiting DS). Yet it is mainly for appearances—the rest of DS is open via a large area in the rear of the office; computer accommodations, document conversion,

Figure 5.1. Stylized Layout of Disability Services at the University of Minnesota–Twin Cities.

interpreter services, student workers, and other office resources are all shared by Student Services and UReturn units, and all 65 DS staff members can easily consult with each other.

UReturn specialists consult frequently with Student Services specialists. This is especially true when employees are taking classes, and Student Services staff are more experienced in providing course-related accommodations. Services for graduate and professional students also require collaboration, since these students are taking classes but are also employees with internships, residencies, teaching positions, or research assistantships. These are handled on a case-by-case basis; one graduate research assistant, for example, may work with Student Services, while another graduate research assistant works with UReturn. Occasionally, UReturn also consults on professional standards for departments—some professions that have licensure, like teaching or nursing, may need to determine standards that all students must meet. In these cases, UReturn can offer an important perspective. Having all disability-related services in one office means students or employees do not have to reregister with a different department when their status as "student" or "employee" changes. Likewise, only one set of medical documentation is needed and is available to specialists in either unit of DS.

In the 2009–2010 academic year, UReturn staff worked with 960 UMN employees with disabilities and medical conditions. Approximately 90 percent were staff, with the biggest percentage working in Facilities Management. The remaining 10 percent were faculty. These ratios are proportional with the campus, where about 10 percent of the UMN's 20,000 employees are faculty.

All UReturn staff provide direct services, the associate director doing 10–20 percent case management, the assistant director at 30 percent case management, and three disability specialists with full-time caseloads. Two administrative assistants provide additional support. DS also is training a contractual employee outside of DS to handle all cases involving DS staff (including staff from UReturn), to reduce any potential conflict of interest. All UReturn staff are generalists, handling all types of disabilities from anywhere on campus, related to both staff and faculty. New cases are rotated among staff. This maintains consistency and increases ease in transferring cases within UReturn, if needed for any reason.

The UMN–Twin Cities campus also coordinates services for faculty and staff at satellite campuses, like Duluth and Crookston. Because of its size, the Duluth campus has a UReturn specialist on-site. All campuses communicate and coordinate with the Twin Cities' UReturn office to ensure consistency and professional support.

Case Management

Determining accommodations is an individual process. Some employees need one-time assistance (e.g., an ergonomic keyboard), and for others, accommodations will be needed for the duration of their employment (e.g., sign language interpreters). For others, the disability may require time off of work and then a period of slowly returning to work. And for still others, the disability may be chronic and episodic requiring assessment periodically. While the university wants someone back to work as quickly as possible, DS helps determine the earliest medically suitable point (e.g., two hours per day for one month, increasing to full time over a period of four months).

Good case management should be very clear in its role: the university can change the *means* by which a job is done, but not the *ends* (the nature of the job or a person's supervisors). Using DS and UReturn is also voluntary; employees with disabilities or health conditions are not required to use them under the law or under UMN policy. It is easier for UReturn staff to work with someone who is not compelled to be there, and therefore skeptical about DS's neutrality or motivations.

Individuals may self-refer, or have a referral from supervisors, HR, the Employee Assistance program, the union, a workers' compensation claim, or due to a short- or long-term disability claim. After an initial intake meeting, UReturn registers the employee. Specialists may contact medical providers for additional information when necessary. Cases may initially be identified as disability-related, an issue related to medical or health conditions, or a type of claim (e.g., workers' compensation), but all case files are commingled, so identifiers and status of cases is flexible. Over 70 percent of appointments with employees occur in work spaces instead of the DS offices. This is essential for determining what a particular job involves, how employees do their work, and the impact of the disability or health condition. After a site visit, consultation occurs with the employee, any related departments or personnel (e.g., Employee Benefits), the employee's supervisor (if necessary), and medical providers. Reasonable accommodations, work adjustments, and any other services are determined and then provided to the employee. If the needed reasonable accommodation has a cost, UReturn has a central budget to use for purchase. This can be very important in expediting the accommodation process in a timely fashion. Follow-up occurs regularly, and any equipment purchased by the university is tracked.

Services may include any of the following:

- Disability-related accommodations (e.g., accessible parking, sign language interpreters, document conversion to accessible formats)
- Preserving the interactive process under disability law
- Referral for counseling
- Equipment purchase or rental
- Facilitation of communication with supervisors or departments
- Job analysis
- Ergonomic evaluations
- Analysis of transferable skills
- Job transfer within the University of Minnesota
- Work adjustment (e.g., change in schedule)
- Referral to community resources, including organizations offering educational materials or information about disabilities and health conditions
- Testifying in arbitration, workers' compensation hearings, or discrimination complaints
- Adjustment counseling

Originally, UReturn did not consider workers' compensation cases or occupational injury and illness cases, but employees with these cases still found their way to DS because the UMN workers' compensation department didn't have an office devoted to disability accommodations. In 2005, UReturn capped a five-year process of integration, and now staff handle all workers' compensation, lost time, and restricted cases. Of the 960 people served last year, 100 were occupational injury or illness cases.

In 2007, the process for handling short-term and long-term cases also changed. The University of Minnesota changed its disability insurance carrier using a request for proposal (RFP) process. UReturn staff were included in the search for companies with a philosophy similar to UReturn and UMN, focused on maintaining human capital and ensuring reasonable accommodations for employees returning to work. The university's new disability insurance company pays for an employee to be embedded in the UReturn office two days each week (at no cost to DS) and to route people to DS when they have benefits claims. With insurance and UReturn staff working closely together, it is easier to identify employees who will need a leave of absence for surgery or a progressive illness. If a leave of absence can be avoided with some basic accommodations or changes in an office to improve access, then the insurance company will pay for those accommodations, minimizing DS and insurance-related costs—a win-win situation.

There are many ways it is beneficial for insurance and UReturn staff to work together. For example, one employee wanted to continue working but was going through treatment for a serious illness; given the nature of her job and strong desire to continue working, UReturn staff recommended that she have a hospital bed at home and be allowed to telecommute. The insurance company paid all related costs, and the employee avoided a lengthy absence from work. She initially worked three hours per day, and then returned to the office full time three months later; this saved three months of employment and benefits because the university allowed her to work from home and helped make related arrangements. In another case, an employee worked with the insurance representative at UReturn, and in consultation with UReturn staff, they realized that accessible parking would solve most of the employee's concerns about work. Since implementing the new insurance policies, the insurance company reported that for every dollar put into the program at DS, the total savings is $28—a worthwhile investment for simple fiscal reasons that do not even take productivity into account.

UReturn is notified in real time when a workers' compensation or disability claim has been identified or if someone's employment status changes while they are on leave. In these situations, UReturn is able to send general information about services to employees who might otherwise never learn about them, who had an opportunity to return to work but didn't realize it, or who simply didn't know DS existed. This outreach is effective at increasing the number of people who use UReturn and in reducing the number of people who slip through the cracks. For example, one professor was hospitalized for several months, and while testing showed there were no problems with her intellect, she wasn't ready to teach in the classroom because she had difficulty with speaking. This employee had no idea UReturn existed, so without coordination with insurers, she typically would have ended up using Social Security Disability Insurance (SSDI) or retiring.

As it currently exists, services for employees with disabilities or health conditions are like a wheel, with UReturn and DS as the hub; services are centralized and decentralized at the same time. UReturn is housed in DS and uses its resources, but staff report to many other UMN units involved in coordination of services, including Risk Management, Occupational Health and Safety, and HR. Services are centralized because there is one office where faculty and staff with disabilities, health conditions, and occupational injuries can go for everything related to disability accommodations and services. It is decentralized because UReturn staff work with so many departments across campus, insurance companies, and so on as an interactive network across campus. Some employees may go to UReturn for issues that should be handled by other units, or for assistance identifying resources and navigating UMN bureacracy; specialists help employees navigate the system and understand their options. While another model would have UReturn staff in each college and in large departments like Facilities Management, this would make it difficult to maintain consistency and neutrality. It also helps in outreach to employees.

New Directions for Higher Education • DOI:10.1002/he

When DS integrated in 2005, staff would frequently have employees coming in after six months of trying to individually negotiate accommodations with supervisors. These employees often "slipped through the cracks" and would be angry with their supervisors, unwilling to return to work or negotiate on accommodations. As UReturn increases its outreach and early intervention, this is happening very rarely.

The main thing is for employees to know they have options and can make decisions about whether they want those services; what's unacceptable is their not knowing services exist. Training deans, administrators, department heads, and supervisors about employee services and UReturn is one way to reach employees, but there is no guarantee employees will disclose disabilities to their supervisors, and people are usually not referred early enough. For UReturn, contacting employees directly improves communication and gets people in the door. Direct communication with employees also makes the campus seem more welcoming for potential and current employees with disabilities, a phenomenon noted at other universities, as well (see, e.g., Patton 2010; Snyder et al. 2010).

As UReturn grows, it faces ongoing challenges of an aging workforce—the UMN median age for the entire employment base is 45, and the median age of faculty is 49 (as compared with a median age of 41 in the U.S. workforce) (U.S. Department of Labor, 2010). With aging, more employees acquire chonic illnesses and health conditions. Like many campuses across the country, there is also limited hiring in the current economy, meaning employees may be asked to do more as coworkers leave and are not replaced. Early intervention becomes even more important, given that existing workers cannot automatically be replaced if they leave or retire.

UReturn seeks to develop a global transitional employment program, which has been successful at a few other universities, including Ohio State University. With this program, employees who are no longer able to do their job (e.g., a mechanic who is unable to lift) would be temporarily placed in another position with the university, with any necessary training (e.g., basic computer skills). Ideally, that employee could be a priority hire for the department, if needed or if the original position is no longer possible. With satellite campuses and continuing possibilities for telecommuting, transitional employment is becoming an important option.

Recommendations for Implementing Employee Services

For campuses that are beginning to address disability services for faculty and staff, there are several important initial considerations:

- Be intentional about where employee services are placed and how they are structured, especially if there are unions on campus. While return-to-work offices can be housed in a number of potential units, consider how the philosophy of the department and perceptions of the department may affect service delivery. For example, DS may be interested in disability law and universal design; general counsel offices would focus on compliance; a benefits office may make cost-effectiveness a priority. Also, campus DS offices usually already have many services in place (e.g., document conversion services, interpreting services), but if the office is small, additional staff with expertise in employment and disability will be necessary.

- Define the process of case management, as well as its scope. The process should be skeletal and flexible, so it can be individualized with each case. Assume that specialists will also spend most of their time on job sites doing job analysis. Personalized good case management based on cornerstones of confidentiality and neutrality can help campuses avoid a polarizing philosophy of services.

- Identify campus resources that will coordinate with Employee Services providers. These may include the Department of Environmental Health and Safety, Ergonomic Health (for workstation evaluations), Human Resources, general counsel's offices, the Employee Assistance program, Employee Benefits, the Employee Wellness program, Employee Career Services, the Office for Conflict Resolution, the Office of Equal Opportunity and Affirmative Action, and the Office of Risk Management and Insurance.

- Create strategies for timely intervention. How will people avail themselves of services at the earliest possible time? If someone's in the hospital, how will employee services be notified and be in contact as soon as the employee is released? Consider case "triage" with workers' compensation, risk management, and other campus offices.

- Join the Disability Management Employer Coalition (DMEC), a national organization that also has state chapters (see website at its http://www.dmec.org/). DMEC includes people from Human Resources, Benefits, Disability Services, and other related campus departments. Members share resources, like policy language and options for site visits. DMEC can also provide professional development on case law related specifically to employment, and legal issues including the Health Insurance Portability and Accountability Act (HIPAA), the Family and Medical Leave Act (FMLA), workers' compensation statutes, Section 504, and the ADA. While Employee Services specialists cannot be experts on the law (because they are not lawyers), specialists should be able to refer employees to the appropriate resources.

Conclusion

This chapter provided an overview of UReturn, the Disability Services unit providing services to UMN faculty and staff with disabilities and health conditions. The physical layout of DS, case management policies, and collaborative work with other UMN departments all emphasize three key ideas:

neutrality, confidentiality, and early intervention. Other campuses may use these as a foundation for implementing employee services and assessing related campus resources. With more students with disabilities graduating from college, an aging workforce, and current economic conditions, employees with disabilities are becoming an increasing part of higher education, and it is more important than ever before that campuses address their needs.

References

Association on Higher Education And Disability (AHEAD). 2010. "Concurrent Sessions, 2010." Accessed December 15, 2010. http://ahead.org/conferences/2010/concurrent.

Baldridge, D. C., and J. F. Veiga. 2006. "The Impact of Anticipated Social Consequences on Recurring Disability Accommodation Requests." *Journal of Management* 32 (1): 158–79.

Harbour, W. S. 2004. *Final Report: The 2004 AHEAD Survey of Higher Education Disability Services Providers.* Waltham, MA: The Association on Higher Education And Disability.

Nafukho, F. M., R. T. Roessler, and K. Kacirek. 2010. "Disability as a Diversity Factor: Implications for Human Resources Practices." *Advances in Developing Human Resources* 12: 395–406.

Patton, J. 2010. "Disability Support." *Occupational Health* 62 (6): 26–27.

Rothstein, L. 2004. "Disability Law and Higher Education: A Road Map for Where We've Been and Where We May Be Heading." *Maryland Law Review* 63: 122–61.

Snyder, L. A., J. S. Carmichael, L. V. Blackwell, J. N. Cleveland, and G. C. Thornton. 2010. "Perceptions of Discrimination and Justice among Employees with Disabilities." *Employee Responsibilities and Rights Journal* 22 (1): 5–19.

U.S. Department of Labor. 2010. "Median Age of the Labor Force by Sex, Race, and Ethnicity, 1978, 1988, 1998, 2008, and projected 2018." Accessed December 15, 2010. http://www.bls.gov/emp/ep_table_306.pdf.

DAVE FUECKER is an Associate Director of Disability Services, coordinating all UReturn services at the University of Minnesota.

WENDY S. HARBOUR is the Lawrence B. Taishoff Professor of Inclusive Education at Syracuse University, where she directs the Taishoff Center for Inclusive Higher Education.

6

The Americans with Disabilities Act Amendments create compelling legal compliance issues, requiring campuswide protocols and coordination.

Legal Challenges and Opportunities

Salome Heyward

For legal issues in the field of disability compliance, this is an exciting time in postsecondary education. The twentieth anniversary of the Americans with Disabilities Act (ADA) signals a reawakening of the commitment to provide equal access to individuals with disabilities. This chapter explores three of the compliance issues that will be of significant importance to colleges and universities for the foreseeable future: the Americans with Disabilities Act Amendments; a call for the adoption of a new service model for individuals with psychiatric disabilities; and the federal government's new emphasis on access to technology.

The ADA Amendments

The Americans with Disabilities Act Amendments Act (ADAAA) resolves the serious problem with the legal interpretation of the definition of disability[1]; however, because of a period of uncertainty regarding agency and judicial interpretations of the new statutory mandates, and the raised expectations of those who anticipate renewed energy devoted to providing access for individuals with disabilities, it will also create some interesting challenges for professionals determining who are "qualified individuals with disabilities" and providing accommodations. There will be a tough battle for the high ground in terms of just how far the obligation to accommodate will be expanded under the redefined definition of *disability,* and postsecondary institutions that do not pay close attention may quickly lose control over their disability services programs with respect to meeting their compliance obligations.

Institutions that wish to avoid becoming participants or casualties in this battle must review and incorporate Amendment mandates from the perspective of what's changed, what remains the same, and the strategies necessary

New Directions for Higher Education, no. 154, Summer 2011 © Wiley Periodicals, Inc.
Published online in Wiley Online Library (wileyonlinelibrary.com) • DOI:10.1002/he.434

to ensure that their accommodation practices and procedures are in line with the new compliance dynamics.

For example, the definition of *disability* in the Amendments still reads, in pertinent part: "a physical or mental impairment that substantially limits a major life activity." Further, courts that have already considered the impact of the Amendments have ruled that case-by-case determinations must still be made, and individuals seeking the protection of the law must still offer "evidence that the extent of the limitations in terms of their own experience . . . is substantial" (see, e.g., *Gil v. Vortex* 2010; *Jenkins v. National Board of Medical Examiners* 2009). Thus, institutions have not lost the right to make disability determinations following examination of information or evidence (i.e., medical documentation) supplied by the individual regarding the disability question.

Another consideration is the mandated broader interpretation of the definition of *disability,* which lowers the threshold for individuals with respect to the amount of proof or evidence that they must offer to establish that they have a disability. The previous restrictive interpretation of the definition has been replaced by a more inclusive presumption of coverage that shifts the focus to the responsibility of institutions to provide meaningful access. Thus, while individuals still must present something more than a diagnosis, the failure to present an exhaustive listing of a condition's manifestations will no longer defeat a disability claim (*Brodsky v. New England School of Law* 2009; *Rohr v. Salt River Project Agricultural Improvement and Power District* 2009).

The proposed Equal Employment Opportunity Commission (EEOC) regulations provide that determinations concerning the definition of *disability* must distinguish between impairments that are consistently considered disabilities and those that may be substantially limiting for some individuals but not others with the same disability. In theory, impairments consistently considered disabilities would require little more than a diagnosis and minimal verification of the functional limitations (e.g., deafness, blindness, cerebral palsy, epilepsy), while the others would require more analysis to determine whether they are substantially limiting for a particular student (e.g., asthma, learning disabilities, back impairments). Thus, what are contemplated are different levels of documentation and scrutiny based on the nature or classification of the impairment.

The Office for Civil Rights (OCR) has ruled that the amount of disability-related information or documentation that is permissible for institutions to obtain is the "minimum information necessary to establish a disability and/or support an accommodation request" (*Central New Mexico Community College* 2007). Thus, there are two legitimate uses for documentation: establishing the existence of a disability, and supporting the need for requested accommodations (e.g., interpreters, extended time on tests, notetakers). Further, the Amendments do not change the definition of *reasonable accommodations.* The amount of information, documentation, and analysis involved in making reasonable accommodation determinations will frequently be greater than that necessary for making a disability determination. Additionally, while the positive impact of disability-related mitigating measures may not be used in making the disability determination, the impact of the measures (both positive and negative) may be used to determine whether the individual is entitled to a reasonable accommodation. (For example, see *Garcia v. State University of New York Health Sciences Center* [2000], a case involving a student who took Ritalin as medication to combat the effects of his attention deficit disorder [ADD]).

The Amendments have not altered the responsibility of individuals to provide documentation supporting the need for all accommodations requested; the right of institutions to refuse to provide accommodations that would fundamentally alter programs and services, or that would impose an undue administrative or financial burden; and/or the right of institutions to provide "equally effective" accommodations to those proposed by the student. The most important information to use from these facts is that:

1. The burden of proof regarding disability determinations has clearly shifted to the institution (i.e., in order to establish that an individual does not meet the definition of disability, an individualized assessment must demonstrate compelling evidence establishing either that there is no impairment, or that the impairment does not substantially limit a major life activity).
2. If evidence concerning the existence of a disability is mixed, it is best to resolve the question in favor of the individual.
3. The disability determination and the reasonable accommodation determination are separate and distinct determinations.

From a legal standpoint, it is important not to succumb to voices that argue that the best approach would be to primarily follow the lead of individuals with disabilities regarding the existence of the disability, and that all requested accommodations must be provided. This is an important pitfall to avoid. Abdicating responsibility to individuals with disabilities and their advocates is not the solution to meeting the compliance obligations of the ADAAA. The obligation of any campus is to provide meaningful access— not to give individuals whatever they think they need or ask for. As many disability service providers know from experience, situations may arise in which what an individual requests and wants is neither reasonable nor the proper accommodation under the circumstances. Therefore, while postsecondary institutions are certainly obligated to consider the preferences or wishes of individuals with disabilities in making these decisions, it is important to remember that, ultimately, the compliance obligation belongs to the institution.

In a related matter, it is important to note that the past practices of licensure boards and testing/certification agencies narrowly and strictly interpreting the definition of disability will present an interesting dilemma for professional and graduate programs. One can anticipate that there will be a significant amount of litigation in this area now that the Amendments are viewed as having leveled the playing field (see, e.g., *Jenkins v. National Board of Medical Examiners* 2009). Previously, professional and graduate schools stood at arm's length and allowed students to fight it out with the boards and agencies. Should the boards and agencies continue to adhere to their past practices, professional schools and graduate programs will need to ask themselves how to respond if students are likely to be denied reasonable accommodations when sitting for professional examinations.

Psychiatric Disabilities

There is growing frustration being expressed by college and university administrators regarding the proper methods to use in managing situations involving individuals with psychiatric disabilities (e.g., depression, schizophrenia, bipolar disorder). Many of these situations are extremely complex and confusing, and as a consequence there are a number of common mistakes that may be made in attempts to balance the competing interests of all parties. This is particularly true concerning students with psychiatric disabilities, who may exhibit behaviors viewed as potentially harmful to themselves or others or incompatible with a learning environment. The following sections consider four specific issues for campuses to consider.

1. *Ignoring Other Pertinent Unique Compliance Issues.* These cases are rarely resolved by answering a straightforward question of compliance. They frequently require that other significant issues be addressed before or at the same time as reasonable accommodation questions. The type of issues that often arise include: health and safety considerations; Family Educational Rights and Privacy Act (FERPA) or ADA confidentiality concerns related to medical inquiries and disclosures; qualified status determinations; and potential disciplinary sanctions. Proper consideration of these issues is necessary to ensure that compliance mandates are satisfied, that individuals receive equitable treatment, and that inadvertent violations of the law are avoided. It generally spells the difference between success and failure in resolving these cases. It is imperative to identify and properly resolve all relevant issues. Examples of questions that consistently arise include:
   - Is this a circumstance where emergency action is warranted?
   - Does the individual's behavior represent a direct threat to the health or safety of self or others?
   - Is there prior evidence of potentially problematic behavior that was not addressed?

- Is the individual's behavior so disruptive that it interferes with the institution's ability to provide educational services and/or the ability of others to benefit from those services?
- Are there reasonable accommodations that would enable the student to meet essential educational or job requirements?

The preceding questions are those that are important to address in these cases, with problems of imminent risk to be considered first. The prevailing standard is that decisions must be supported by objective medical evidence and/or a clear pattern of behavior, and be logical, reasonable, and free from bias and discrimination.

2. *Treating Psychiatric Conditions or Disabilities Differently from Other Disabilities.* It is not uncommon for individuals with psychiatric disabilities to argue that the manifestations of the disability that are troubling or disruptive should be excused, ignored, or worked around as an accommodation itself. Further, there are many examples of institutional administrators who have not acted under circumstances that clearly call for action because they believed that doing so would violate statutory rights and protections provided to individuals with disabilities. Each of these opinions is representative of the mistaken belief that disability status trumps all other considerations. The fact that an individual has a disability does not shield him or her from the consequences of inappropriate and/or dangerous conduct or behavior (see, e.g., *Concepcion v. Commonwealth of Puerto Rico* 2010; *DeSales University* 2005). The EEOC, OCR, and the courts have consistently ruled that postsecondary institutions are entitled to take appropriate action under circumstances where (a) a significant imminent risk exists; (b) the individual's behavior is a direct threat to the health and safety of self or other and/or is so disruptive that it interferes with the institution's ability to provide educational services; (c) the individual is judged not to be a qualified individual (e.g., is not able to meet core requirements of the college or degree program, even with accommodations); and (d) the standards applied are equal to those applied to other similarly situated individuals.

3. *Basing Decisions on Generalizations Regarding the Psychiatric Condition.* It is not uncommon for the mere existence of the psychiatric condition or disability to influence the decision making of institution officials, rather than the actual circumstances that give rise to a situation demanding action. For example, such generalizations may arise from (a) the use of experts who have not evaluated the individual and/or reviewed his or her medical records; (b) discussion about the limitations and/or behavioral symptoms that most people with the condition have rather than the individual's specific functional limitations; and (c) speculation concerning how or whether the particular psychiatric condition would impact success without consideration of the individual's actual circumstances. What is required is an individualized assessment, instead

of generalized stereotypes regarding the impairment/disability (*Mastrolillo v. State of Connecticut* 2009; *University of Cincinnati* 2006). An individualized objective assessment must focus on all circumstances relevant to the individual's ability to participate in an educational program. Proper determinations involve consideration of objective medical evidence concerning the individual's impairment, as well as reliable information concerning the impact of the individual's functional limitations relative to pertinent requirements of the program or job, the individual's performance and behavior in the environment, and the availability of reasonable accommodations.

4. *Failing to Involve Necessary Experts and/or to Provide Due Process.* Many of these cases involve students in academic crisis, or students subject to disciplinary sanctions, where faculty members or students are called upon to make decisions concerning whether the student should be suspended or dismissed. Frequently (and this is a particular problem for graduate and professional programs), decisions are made without participation or input from disability experts, as well as a full understanding of the institution's compliance obligations through consultation with general counsel and/or the campus ADA/504 coordinator. Making and enforcing unilateral actions or decisions that have an adverse impact on the participation of students with disabilities is not a wise way to do business. Final decisions that deprive, or have a substantial impact on, the rights or opportunities of students with disabilities must include proper due process procedures (*Marietta College* 2005; *Mastrolillo v. State of Connecticut* 2009; *University of Cincinnati* 2006). Essential due process provisions include notice of the information and evidence that is being considered, an opportunity for the student to be heard and to present evidence, notice of decisions and explanations regarding the proposed or recommended actions, and an opportunity to appeal. Further, the institution must be able to demonstrate that the standards or requirements being enforced, as well as any sanctions being applied, are the same as those applicable to similarly situated nondisabled students.

While the procedural mistakes discussed above certainly reflect a basic lack of understanding regarding the compliance obligations that must be met, on a broader scale they are symptomatic of a much larger problem and a substantially greater challenge facing postsecondary institutions. They signal a compelling need for colleges and universities to adopt a new service model for interacting with individuals with psychiatric disabilities. The traditional model employed by many institutions primarily consists of offering counseling for minor to moderate academic stress–related situations, typically focused on changing student behaviors. However, on the accommodation side, the approach tends to fluctuate between two extremes: providing any and all accommodations requested, or using the mere existence of the disability to justify a determination that the individual is not qualified. Additionally, the most serious psychiatric issues tend to be referred out, ignored until they reach crisis portions, and/or left to campus security to manage (see, e.g., *College of Marin* 2006; *Shin v. University of Maryland Medical System* 2010; *Toledo v. University of Puerto Rico* 2008; *University of Cincinnati* 2006). These approaches are best characterized as passive, reactionary, and ineffectual.

Clearly, the traditional service model is broken. The educational landscape has significantly changed, and institutions have failed to update their administrative approach to keep pace with the realities of this new landscape. These realties include substantial increase in the number of students with documented serious psychiatric disabilities enrolling in colleges and universities, and a student profile that increasingly looks less like the traditional 18- to 22-year-old student with limited life experience. The average student population today includes employees who have been downsized, military veterans on the GI Bill, empty nesters, mid-twenties GED recipients, first-generation college enrollees, high school graduates who received special education services, and individuals who have been primarily home schooled. Tragedies including those at Virginia Tech and the University of Alabama raise serious questions regarding the ability of institutions to address significant health and safety challenges in academic environments.

These are realities that require more than the passive, reactionary, and ineffectual strategies of the past, making a compelling argument for the adoption of a new model of service delivery for students with psychiatric disabilities. While reasonable people will engage in spirited debates about what the new model should look like, professional experience and respected organizations (see, e.g., JED Foundation 2008) tells us that important key strategies are:

- Use of an intervention team that includes qualified mental health professionals (those capable of diagnosing and treating serious psychiatric conditions), as well as disability, security, and legal experts, to take the lead in complex cases (e.g., emergency situations, cases of direct threat, situations where conditions are imposed on the individual's participation based on his or her disability). The team would be charged with the responsibility to take the lead in managing such cases.
- Developing methods of administration to ensure that those making decisions that potentially have an adverse impact on individuals with disabilities (academic standing committees, disciplinary proceedings, etc.) have access to appropriate experts to ensure that proper standards are applied. For example, a FERPA expert would provide guidance if medical inquiries and disclosures are at issue, an ADA/504 coordinator might answer questions regarding the standards for establishing a "direct threat," and a mental health expert would evaluate the medical information and provide input concerning the manifestations of the individual's condition.

- Develop proper protocols for clinical rotations, internships, and extern-ships that address potential health and safety issues and the circumstances under which a student's participation may be restricted or denied. The protocols should incorporate the compliance standard identified by OCR (i.e., valid evidence that the student's conduct has the reasonably fore-seeable potential to harm clients in clinical, medical, counseling, or other similar programs [*North Central Technical College* 1997]).
- Modify disability accommodation procedures to ensure that the input of mental health experts is sought when requested accommodations raise issues of academic integrity and qualified status.
- Identify the circumstances in which individuals with disabilities are enti-tled to due process, and ensure that proper procedures are in place and adequate notice is provided about their rights to appeal decisions.

Access to Technology

There was considerable regulatory activity in 2010 that indicates that the federal government has shifted compliance attention to ensuring that post-secondary institutions and businesses provide equal access to technology for individuals with disabilities. For example, when a pilot program between Amazon.com and a number of postsecondary institutions involved the use of the Kindle DX (an electronic book reader) in place of textbooks, this resulted in Justice Department settlement agreements and a lawsuit being filed (U.S. Department of Justice [DOJ] 2010a, 2010b). The controversy was that the Kindle DX was not fully accessible to students who were blind and had low vision, with no adaptive technology access to the menu and navi-gational controls of the device. Following the settlement on June 29, 2010, the DOJ and the U.S. Department of Education (DOE) issued a joint letter to all college and university presidents in which the agencies reminded them of their obligations to provide equal opportunity to technology and to ensure that emerging technology includes access to individuals with disabilities.

Three other key pieces of legislation have also passed. On July 26, 2010, the House of Representatives approved legislation to ensure full access for individuals with disabilities to the Internet and television, and the DOJ issued advance notice regarding proposed rulemaking concerning accessi-bility of Web information and services. In addition, the final regulations revising Title II and Title III of the ADA were published on September 15, 2010. The regulations will take effect six months after they are published in the *Federal Register*. A significant portion of the regulations addresses the obligation to ensure that individuals with disabilities are provided effective communication, including an expanded list of auxiliary aids and services with emphasis on the use of adaptive technology. Finally, the Higher Edu-cation Opportunity Act of 2008 includes a number of provisions concern-ing access to technology (e.g., the establishment of advisory commissions on adaptive technology and on accessible instructional materials in post-secondary education for students with disabilities).

These developments make it imperative that postsecondary institutions review their program accessibility standards to ensure that they are adequate for meeting the obligation to provide access to technology. The standard in the law is that individuals with disabilities must be provided aids, services, and benefits equally effective to those provided nondisabled individuals (34 C.F.R. Section 104.4(b)(iii) and 28 C.F.R. Section 35.150(a)). "An important indicator regarding the extent to which a public [entity] is obligated to utilize adaptive technology is the degree to which it is relying on technology to serve its nondisabled patrons" (*California State University* 1997). It is significant that in the Kindle DX situation, the institutions were not permitted to use technology under circumstances in which access was restricted for individuals with disabilities. This makes it clear that adopting and using technology advances without thought or consideration of the limited access afforded individuals with disabilities is unacceptable.

In keeping with these new developments, institutions should ensure that they have effective accessibility standards and guidelines in place to address access to technology for the full range of programs and services offered. This would include institutional websites, library resources and services, instructional services, and computer labs and workstations. Further, appropriate standards in the field, such as the Section 508 Accessibility Standards and Web Content Accessibility Guidelines (WCAG) should be consulted for checkpoints for eliminating absolute and substantial barriers to access.

Summary

Going forward, the challenge for postsecondary institutions will be to understand the compliance imperatives that are a necessary consequence of the developments discussed in this chapter. Specifically, the expanded definition of *disability* will require a willingness to consider any and all information available to answer the question of whether a student's claim of the existence of a disability is valid as well as an awareness that there must be a compelling reason to seek additional documentation where a student has provided evidence of a diagnosis by a qualified professional and a consistent history of having been accommodated with respect to the disability in question. In addition, the increasing numbers of individuals with psychiatric disabilities in the postsecondary environment have created a need for a new service model that focuses on (a) provision of effective mental health services; (b) proper management of issues of disclosure, privacy, and confidentiality; (c) protocols for addressing health and safety concerns; and (d) offering effective accommodations for individuals with psychiatric disabilities. Finally, technology will increasingly become the primary vehicle for delivery of educational services and, as such, colleges and universities

NEW DIRECTIONS FOR HIGHER EDUCATION • DOI:10.1002/he

must adopt a proactive approach to providing equal and meaningful access to individuals with disabilities.

Note

1. Individuals who are entitled to protection from discrimination under the Americans with Disabilities Act (ADA) are "qualified individuals with a disability" (42 U.S.C. 12112(a)). The ADA defines *disability,* in pertinent part, as "a physical or mental impairment that substantially limits one or more of the major life activities of such individual" (42 U.S.C. 12102(2)). After more than 20 years of enforcement, the legal interpretation of the term *disability* by federal courts, including the Supreme Court, had "narrowed the broad scope of protection intended to be afforded by the ADA, thus eliminating protection for many individuals whom Congress intended to protect" (Pub. L. No. 110-325, 122 Stat. 3553 (2008)). Thus, the Americans with Disabilities Act Amendments Act (ADAAA) was passed to clarify congressional intent to: broadly construe the term *disability;* to expand the categories of individuals entitled to protection under the act; and to eliminate the "inappropriately high level of limitation necessary to obtain coverage under the ADA" imposed by previous court decisions (122 Stat. at 3553–56).

References

Brodsky v. New England School of Law, 617 F. Supp. 2d 1 (D.C. M.A. 2009).
California State University, 11 NDLR 71 (April 1997).
Central New Mexico Community College, 37 NDLR 186 (August 2007).
College of Marin, 35 NDLR 177 (June 2006).
Concepcion v. Commonwealth of Puerto Rico, 08-2378 (FAB) (D.C. P.R. 2010).
DeSales University, 32 NDLR 150 (February 2005).
Garcia v. State University of New York Health Sciences Center, 19 NDLR 57 (E.D.N.Y., 2000).
Gil v. Vortex, 09-11993-RGS (D.C. M.A. 2010).
JED Foundation. 2008. *Student Mental Health and the Law.* New York: JED Foundation.
Jenkins v. National Board of Medical Examiners, 08-5371(6th Cir. 2009).
Marietta College, 31 NDLR 23 (July 2005).
Mastrolillo v. State of Connecticut, 352 Fed. Appx. 472 (2nd Cir. 2009).
North Central Technical College, 11 NDLR 326 (June 1997).
Rohr v. Salt River Project Agricultural Improvement and Power District, 555 F.3d 850 (9th Cir. 2009).
Shin v. University of Maryland Medical System, 09-1126 (4th Cir. 2010).
Toledo v. University of Puerto Rico, 01-1980 (SEC)(D.C.P.R. 2008).
University of Cincinnati, 35 NDLR 151 (April 2006).
U.S. Department of Justice. 2010a, January. "Press Releases." Washington, DC: U.S. Department of Justice.
U.S. Department of Justice. 2010b, March 24. "Letter of Resolution." Washington, DC: U.S. Department of Justice.

SALOME HEYWARD *is a civil rights attorney specializing in disability discrimination law and disability management. She is President of Salome Heyward and Associates.*

NEW DIRECTIONS FOR HIGHER EDUCATION • DOI:10.1002/he

7

A proactive risk management approach focuses on both academic and cocurricular needs to ensure disability services will maintain the best interests of students with disabilities, the broader campus community, and the institution.

Responding to and Supporting Students with Disabilities: Risk Management Considerations

Anne Lundquist, Allan Shackelford

A wide variety of risk management issues are present every day on campuses across this country, many of which can arise from unexpected sources and situations. However, a 2004 survey showed that, at that time, few of the major colleges and universities responding to the survey had a comprehensive risk or crisis management plan in place (Mitroff, Diamond, and Alpasian 2006). Awareness has increased somewhat since then, in large part because of the attention and reactions prompted by several devastating human tragedies and natural disasters at a number of colleges and universities. But the impact of that change appears somewhat mixed. The National Association of College and University Business Officers' (NACUBO) National Campus Safety and Security Project survey reported that 85 percent of campuses have emergency preparedness plans that cover a wide array of possible emergencies (NACUBO 2009). However, that same year a survey by the Association of Governing Boards of Universities and Colleges (AGB) and United Educators noted that 60 percent of respondents said their institutions do not use comprehensive, strategic risk-assessment to identify major risks to mission success (AGB 2009). According to Whitfield (2003), "while commitment to risk management is strong, actual execution continues to evolve and remains weak" (17).

Recognition that this issue is of particular importance to the effective operation of disability services has just recently begun to receive the attention it demands. In view of factors affecting the environment in which higher education finds itself today, administrators should make it a high priority to understand how potentially complex risk and liability issues can significantly challenge and impact decisions within the context of disability services.

NEW DIRECTIONS FOR HIGHER EDUCATION, no. 154, Summer 2011 © Wiley Periodicals, Inc.
Published online in Wiley Online Library (wileyonlinelibrary.com) • DOI:10.1002/he.435

Legal Considerations in Higher Education

Historically, colleges and universities have been viewed as ivory towers surrounded by reality. The world of higher education was largely a self-created, self-perpetuating, insular, isolated, and self-regulating environment. In this organizational culture, institutions were generally governed under the traditional, independent "silos of power and silence" management model, with the right hand in one administrative area or unit often unaware of the left hand's mission, objectives, programs, practices, and contributions in another unit.

For a significant period of time in our nation's history, the outside world intruded upon colleges and universities by invitation only and higher education faced few legal requirements. For many years, courts and legislatures generally deferred to decisions made by the academy. One such example was the 1928 *Anthony v. Syracuse* court decision that upheld the dismissal of a Syracuse student based simply on the rationale that she was not a "typical Syracuse girl" (*Anthony v. Syracuse* 1928).

The 1960s brought significant societal changes and saw the federal government begin to enact specific legislation affecting colleges and universities. The proliferation of federal laws, coupled with the rise of aggressive consumerism toward the end of the 1990s, led to an increased risk of private legal claims against institutions of higher education—and their administrators—by individuals or groups of students. Higher education has lost its special status and is now treated like any other business by judges, juries, and creative plaintiffs' attorneys. In the summer of 2008, for example, the University of Nevada at Reno was defending more than 30 pending lawsuits and had spent $1.7 million on outside counsel for just four of these cases (Schmidt 2009).

Furthermore, the trend in claims against institutions of higher education is for courts to determine that a "special relationship" exists between the institution and the harmed party (in most cases a student or students), and then to review and evaluate the institution's decisions and actions against this standard. This has led courts from finding that colleges and universities owed "no duty" to those harmed in a higher education setting, to instead reviewing and evaluating the "reasonableness" of campus decisions and actions based on the "foreseeability" of the consequences as the threshold question in evaluating legal claims and allegations. Courts are interpreting this "special relationship" between institutions of higher education and students as imposing a legally mandated duty on colleges and universities to take necessary and appropriate steps to protect students in their care. Lake (2007) opined that, in the future, colleges and universities will be legally called to account for their actions more frequently. Specifically, he states that, while institutions of higher education may not be held liable more frequently, they will now "have to go to court, the legislatures, and Congress and explain why [they] did what [they] did—or did not do—more consistently and more probingly than ever before" (Lake 2007, 43).

NEW DIRECTIONS FOR HIGHER EDUCATION • DOI:10.1002/he

In today's landscape, claims can be brought against colleges and universities for any number of things including (but not limited to): tort litigation (negligence, gross negligence, personal injury, property damage, premises liability); breach of contract; negligent supervision; and failure to provide constitutional and/or contractual due process. While it may be impossible to anticipate, react, and defend against all such claims, there are proactive and responsible steps that colleges and universities can take to reduce their risk of litigation and possible liability, while simultaneously providing appropriate support services and programs to all students, especially those students with disabilities and, in particular, those with significant psychological issues.

Risk Management: The Context for Disability Services

Risk for an institution of higher education can come in many forms: physical or emotional harm to students, faculty, or staff; financial losses; or damage to facilities or reputation. There are a variety of possible responses to particular types of risk: avoid or ignore it; attempt to transfer it to a third party; make attempts to reduce, mitigate, or control the negative effects; or, in some instances, decide to accept some or all of the consequences of the risk. Obviously, we do not have the option of ignoring the risks potentially posed by having students on our campuses who have disabilities, including significant psychiatric disabilities. Moreover, the focus of risk management in the higher education setting should not be simply to avoid lawsuits and legal liability. The intent and focus should be to protect students, faculty, staff, and visitors from reasonably foreseeable harm by reducing unnecessary risk. As Achampong (2010) summarized, "In the final analysis, the ultimate goal of efforts to maximize an institution's value (through risk management) . . . is the achievement of the institution's expressed vision" (23).

Within this context, "risk management" is clearly a disability services issue. There may be certain threats inherent in the presence of particular students on campus—who may be known or unknown to the disability services office. The risk can relate to the specific nature of a student's disability and the behaviors associated with the disability that, under certain circumstances, may pose a threat to the student or to others. In every instance, the best interests and legal rights of a particular student involved must be considered and addressed, as well as those of other students, the campus community generally and the institution itself. As Novak and Paterson (2009) noted: "Key court decisions . . . imply that the responsibility of the university is to not only enforce standards of conduct and safety protocols but also to engage in proactively addressing known behaviors or environments that may result in harm or injury to students" (6).

Certainly, not all students with disabilities pose a threat of harm to themselves or others, and not all students who may pose a potential threat have diagnosed or documented disabilities. But, especially as more students with significant mental health issues enter higher education, disability services providers (as well as student affairs professionals, support staff, advisors, and faculty members) are spending more time dealing with and responding to the behavioral issues that can arise. As responsible administrators, it is important to be well-versed not only in the best practices for providing accommodations to students with psychological disabilities, but also in the processes, procedures, and best practices that provide legal protection for the institution and result in a healthy educational, co-curricular, and residential living environment for all students and a safe and secure environment for everyone who is a member of the campus community.

Lessons Learned

In recent years, courts have intervened to second-guess or weigh in on the appropriateness of an institution's decisions and actions when faced with the complex challenge of responding to students who presented a risk to themselves or others. In 2002, the parents of Elizabeth Shin sued MIT for $27 million for the suicide death of their daughter and later settled for an undisclosed sum (Richards 2007). A federal trial court in Virginia found that Ferrum College had owed a "duty of care" to a student who hanged himself. The court determined that there was a "duty to protect" based on the institution's "special relationship" with its students (*Schieszler v. Ferrum college* 2002). In view of this, many institutions have chosen to respond more aggressively, not only by providing an increased range of psychologically related support services and programs, but also by developing and implementing specific policies to address issues regarding possible self-harm or endangerment. These efforts can protect not only the troubled student, but others at the institution.

In some instances, however, these policies have not withstood legal challenge. For example, in 2006, Hunter College removed a student from the residence halls after the student sought treatment following a suicide attempt. Their school policy stated: "Any student who attempts suicide or in any way attempts to harm him or herself will be asked to take a leave of absence for at least one semester from the residence hall and will be evaluated by the school psychologist or his/her designated counselor prior to returning to the residence hall" (*Doe v. Hunter College* 2004). The student claimed that the policy violated the Fair Housing Act, the Americans with Disabilities Act, and Section 504 of the Rehabilitation Act. The school settled the case for $165,000 (Capriccioso 2006).

In a similar situation, a student at George Washington University was forced to withdraw and was banned from campus after checking himself into a university hospital for depression. The University sent him a letter stating that he had violated the student conduct code by engaging in "endangering behavior" (Kinzie 2006). While these institutions and others may have had the best interests of students in mind in enacting these policies, the overreaction scenarios they created had a detrimental effect on the individual students involved, as well as proving to be potentially discriminatory against students with apparent mental health issues.

Of course, colleges and universities can also be held responsible in the court of public opinion for not taking action when warning signs appear obvious. Such has been true regarding Virginia Tech following the release of the Virginia Tech Review Panel's report which listed ten separate documented episodes of threatening behavior by Seung-Hui Cho prior to the April 16, 2007, shootings that resulted in the deaths of 32 innocent victims. Moreover, several key administrators and staff members had specific knowledge about Cho's threatening behaviors, but were under the impression, supported by their legal counsel, that they could not share such information with one another, intervene, and take action ("Mass Shootings at Virginia Tech" 2007). It is likely that much more damaging information will come to light regarding the failure of Virginia Tech administrators to take appropriate steps to respond to a known threat. On April 16, 2009, the families of two students who were killed, and had not entered into a previous settlement agreement, filed lawsuits against the Commonwealth of Virginia, Virginia Tech, and individual administrators and counselors. Each seeks $10 million in damages.

On three occasions, most recently November 22, 2010, the Virginia trial court judge ruled that claims of gross negligence will be allowed to proceed against the university, its president, a former executive vice president, and three employees of the university's counseling center ("Virginia Tech Officials Can be Sued Over '07 Shooting Deaths" 2010).

Responding Effectively Means Planning Proactively

As the previous examples indicate, the current legal landscape can make appropriate decision making by college and university administrators complex and difficult. Administrators and staff can be confused by the law and often face the dilemma of under- versus overresponse. At the same time, students may face the choice of seeking support and assistance for their disabilities or mental illnesses, or potentially jeopardizing their educational opportunities merely by seeking help and making their particular situation known. Under these circumstances, it is especially important that disability services providers be part of institution-wide risk management planning, assessment, and preparation.

It is also important to recognize that institutional risks and crisis management scenarios often require decision makers to balance competing needs and demands, both internal and external. A behavioral issue involving a student who poses a threat to self or others may involve the varying agendas of students, parents, faculty, staff, alumni, as well as lawyers, insurance brokers, community members, the press and media, and governmental investigative and enforcement agencies. Developing effective review, assessment, and decision-making strategies, as well as determining the roles and responsibilities of key decision makers, is critical to minimizing risk and controlling the outcome of such scenarios.

Over the past several years, numerous institutions have faced situations where the risk incurred and the resulting consequences were almost unimaginable and, certainly, in some cases, unforeseeable. However, in response to expected or unexpected crises, whether resulting from the uncontrollable force of nature or from an unfortunate student-generated human tragedy, there are some common themes for those institutions that fared well and responded effectively and appropriately versus those that did not. Below are listed characteristics of an effective response.

- Procedures and protocols had been developed and implemented in advance of the crisis scenario and their application, use, and effectiveness had been tested under controlled circumstances.
- The senior leadership team was responsive, creative, and decisive and exhibited flexibility as unforeseen situations and circumstances developed or became known.
- Administrators made decisions in keeping with their existing protocols and procedures and did not respond idiosyncratically to "the crisis."
- Decisions and action steps were reevaluated as new information became available.

The following characteristics were associated with an inadequate response:

- Institutional policies, protocols, and procedures were either lacking or shown to be insufficient and ineffective.
- Institutional policies and administrative decisions were apparently based on subjective stereotypes and not an objective analysis of a particular situation.
- Senior administrators were aware of relevant, important information in advance of the incident, but failed to act or intervene.
- Key administrators did not communicate effectively with each other and/or covered up unflattering information regarding their areas of responsibility.
- The press and media came early and often and the institution seemed unprepared to respond and unable to control its message.
- Administrative decisions, intentional or otherwise, of what "not to do" were often more important to the outcomes than decisions regarding what "to do."

Practical Considerations: Risk Management Protocols

All experienced disability service providers are well aware of the legal mandates imposed by Section 504 of the Rehabilitation Act of 1973, the Americans with Disabilities Act, and their related amendments (the Americans with Disabilities Act Amendments Act). They know that a "disability" is a physical or mental impairment that substantially limits one or more major life activity and that an "otherwise qualified" person must be provided "reasonable" accommodations. But the devil is often in the details, especially when it comes to dealing with students who may pose a risk of harm to themselves or others.

Sometimes, there can be more questions than answers. For example:

- Does a particular student have a disability—or not?
- Is the institution "on notice" that a student has a disability?
- For students who pose a risk of harm to self or others, and may have a disclosed psychological disability, what are the legal hurdles to assist them and/or remove them from campus?
- If there is a threat of harmful behavior, what are the institution's legal duties and responsibilities?
- Is the assessment of risk based solely on an objective analysis or has subjectivity entered into the process?

The obligation and duty to respond to a student who poses a threat to self or others is fairly clear under federal law.[1] However, as the facts and circumstances surrounding the recent tragedy in Tucson have pointed-out, an institution's related obligations and duties under the laws of a particular state may be open to interpretation.

The Office for Civil Rights (OCR) has ruled that federal law does not prevent an institution from addressing the dangers posed by an individual who represents a "direct threat" even if she or he is a person with a disability, as that person may no longer be qualified for a particular educational program. In their letter to Bluffton University, the OCR noted: "Nothing in Section 504 prevents educational institutions from addressing the dangers posed by an individual who represents a 'direct threat' to the health and safety of self or others, even if such an individual is a person with a disability, as that individual may no longer be qualified for a particular educational program or activity" (*OCR Letter: Bluffton* 2004). The OCR cautioned, however, that institutions of higher education must take steps to ensure that any disciplinary actions against a person posing a threat "are not a pretext or excuse for discrimination." The OCR further noted in its letter to Marietta College that it is incumbent upon colleges and universities to adhere to fair due process procedures including giving the student notice and an opportunity to address the information and evidence to the extent practicable (*OCR Letter: Marietta* 2005).

The updates to the Family Educational Rights and Privacy Act (FERPA) in January 2009 make it clear that an "educational agency or institution may disclose information to an eligible student's parents in a health or safety emergency." The new regulations, in fact, encourage institutions to release information to avoid outbreaks of violence and they allow the institution to take into consideration the "totality of the circumstances" regarding the "significant and particular threat." As stated in the regulations, the Department of Education will not "substitute its judgment for that of the educational agency or institution in evaluating the circumstances making its determination" (FERPA 2009).

While institutions of higher education may intervene and remove students from campus if they pose a direct threat to self or others, it is important to consider each case individually and to have the appropriate administrators and decision-makers involved in each instance make the best decision for the particular student as well as for the institution as a whole. At their core, these policies have a primary desire to protect a student from self-harm or to protect the community from the negative effects of self-injurious behavior, but what is legally permissible and what is "the best decision" for the student and institution may not always coincide (Bombardieri 2006). But Pavela (as cited in Capriccioso 2006), warns against establishing "hair trigger" removal policies for students who threaten suicide or harm to others. Pavela also notes: "Our primary job is to educate students, not devise creative ways to dismiss them".

So how does an institution effectively go about making these difficult decisions? Following guidance from the OCR, recent court cases and best practices in student development for responding to students with disabilities, the following protocols should be in place:

1. *Establish a Threat Assessment Team.* Campus threat assessment teams are critical in today's legal and risk management landscape. They are not only necessary in terms of preparation and planning for major campus incidents (such as weather-related disasters, active shooting situations, or hazardous materials spills), but also in terms of dealing with and responding to the day-to-day incidents that, when dealt with proactively and properly, can prevent future harm or tragedy. Disability service providers should be integral members of such teams and should be included in decision making not only about individual student issues, but also about overarching institutional planning efforts. Lake (2007) notes the importance of such teams:

   > Dangerous people rarely show all of their symptoms to just one department or group on campus. A professor may see a problem in an essay, the campus police may endure belligerent statements, a resident assistant may notice the student is a loner, the counseling center may notice that the student fails to appear for a follow-up visit. Acting independently, no department is likely to solve the problem. In short, college must recognize that managing an educational environment is a team effort, calling for collaboration and multilateral solutions. (43)

2. *Utilize Individualized, Direct Threat Assessment in Decision Making.* OCR has provided comprehensive guidance to colleges and universities regarding the appropriate response to students who exhibit dangerous or threatening behavior. The OCR makes it clear that decisions made in the best interest of the individual student involved, as well as the institution as a whole, should be made based on observed behaviors and specific conduct, not beliefs or suppositions about the cause of the behaviors (or the alleged or documented diagnosis). Decision makers should obtain credible medical evidence, diagnoses, and opinions from qualified medical professionals and use that information for assessment and decision making. To the extent practicable, the institution should provide notice to the student about impending decisions regarding his or her enrollment, afford the student an opportunity to be heard, and provide relevant, supporting information. It is also important to assess the actual risk of imminent harm using the direct threat analysis. Key decision makers should review the nature, frequency, and duration of the behavior and attempt to assess the likelihood, imminence, and nature of the harmful conduct in the future.

3. *Consider Alternatives to Suspension or Withdrawal.* Even if the ultimate decision in a particular student's situation is for that individual to be removed from the college or university's campus, it is important, as a part of the interactive discussion, review, and decision-making process, to consider other alternatives. This will ensure that the student can provide proposed solutions that administrators may not yet have considered and may allow for the student to continue his or her education in a modified fashion. Such alternatives can include releasing a student from campus housing, proposing a medical leave of absence for a semester or more, allowing a reduced class load, or developing a process by which a student can complete his or her coursework online or from a distance.

4. *Establish and Communicate Conditions and Requirements for Return.* If the decision has been made for the student to leave the institution (either voluntarily or involuntarily), it is important to establish clear parameters and conditions for the student's return. More stringent requirements for readmission can be established and put in place than in the original admissions process and all requirements should be clearly outlined in writing to the student, with copies to all administrators at the institution who have a legitimate educational interest. Readmission agreements should state the terms of exit and the reason, indicate what medical information is required to consider readmission, state that the institution desires to assist and support the student, but has certain expectations with which the student must comply, including asking various health care providers to confirm counseling or other relevant medical treatment.

5. *Establish Clear Parameters for Information Sharing with Key Administrators.* FERPA establishes guidelines for the sharing of information

about a student. It is permissive in terms of how that information can be shared, so each institution should establish more clearly its own internal rules and policies and state the ways in which information can be shared, and with whom. The legislation makes it clear that those with a "legitimate educational interest" include those who perform an administrative task as outlined in the person's official job duties or who perform a supervisory or instructional task directly related to the student's education. It may also include those who perform a service or benefit for the student such as health care, job placement, financial aid, or other related areas (§99.36 (b) (1) and (2)). It is up to each institution to establish a clear policy and protocol for determining which persons have a "need to know" in relationship to particular student issues.

Conclusion

Making the "right" risk management decisions involving students with significant psychological disabilities requires, of course, a clear and comprehensive understanding of the legal obligations and duties at issue. It also requires taking into consideration the best interests of these individual students. At the same time, decision makers must focus on the best interests of students generally, other potentially affected members of the campus community, as well as the best interests, mission, values, reputation, and security of the institution.

Note

1. This article was written prior to the shooting tragedy in Tucson. While the relevant issues remain clear under federal law, the facts and circumstances surrounding this incident have pointed out that an institution's related obligations and duties under the laws of a particular state may be open to interpretation.

References

Achampong, F. 2010. "Integrating Risk Management and Strategic Planning." *Planning for Higher Education* 38 (2): 22–27.

Anthony v. Syracuse, 224 App. Div. 487, 231 N.Y.S. 435 (N.Y. App. Div. 1928).

Association of Governing Boards of Universities and Colleges (AGB). 2009. *The state of enterprise risk management at colleges and universities today.* Accessed September 26, 2010. http://www.agb.org/reports/2009/state-enterprise-risk-management-colleges-and-universities-today.

Bombardieri, M. 2006. "Parents Strike Settlement with MIT after Death of Daughter." *Boston Globe*, April 4, n.p. Accessed July 25, 2010. http://www.boston.com/news/local/articles/2006/04/04/parents_strike_settlement_with_mit_in_death_of_daughter/.

Capriccioso, R. 2006, August 24. "Hunter Settles Suicide Suit." *Inside Higher Education*. Accessed July 27, 2010. http://www.insidehighereducation.com.

Doe v. Hunter College, 04-Civ-6470, 9 (S.D.N.Y. 2004)(second amended complaint). Accessed October 26, 2010. http://www.bazelon.org/issues/education/incourt/Hunter/courtdocs.html.

Family Educational Rights and Privacy Act (FERPA) 2009. (20 U.S.C. § 1232g; 34 CFR Part 99).

Kinzie, S. 2006, March 10. "GWU Suit Prompts Questions of Liability." *The Washington Post.* Accessed August 2, 2010. http://www.washingtonpost.com/wp-dyn/content/article /2006/03/09/AR2006030902550.html.

Lake, P. F. 2007, June 29. "Higher Education Called to Account: Colleges and the Law After Virginia Tech." *Chronicle of Higher Education* 43.

"Mass Shootings at Virginia Tech." 2007. Report of the Review Panel, presented to Governor Kane, Commonwealth of Virginia. Accessed January 12, 2009. http://www .vtreviewpanel.org/.

Mitroff, I. I., M. A. Diamond, and C. M. Alpasian. 2006. "How Prepared Are America's Colleges and Universities for Major Crises? *Change.* Accessed April 30, 2008. http://www.scup.org/knowledge/crisis_planning/diamond.html.

National Association of College and University Business Officers (NACUBO), National Campus Safety and Security Project. 2009. Washington, DC: NACUBO. Accessed October 26, 2010. http://www.nacubo.org/Documents/Initiatives/CSSPSurvey Results.pdf.

Novak, K., and B. Paterson. 2009. "Reframing Campus Conduct: Integrating Risk Reduction Strategies into Campus Conduct Systems." Burlington: University of Vermont. Accessed July 21, 2010. http://learn.uvm.edu/legal/manual/novak_kim_risk_reduction_ session_manuscript.pdf.

OCR Letter: Bluffton University. 2004. OCR Complaint # 15–04–2042–2004. Accessed July 25, 2010. http://www.bcm.edu/ilru/dlrp/html/topical/FAPSI/OCR/bluffton.html.

OCR Letter: Marietta College. 2005, March 18. OCR Complaint # 15–04–2060 2005. Accessed July 25, 2010. http://www.nacua.org/meetings/virtualseminars/october2005 /Documents/MariettaCollegeOCRComplaint.pdf.

Richards, S. E. 2007, March 9. "The Suicide Test" Accessed July 27, 2010. www.jed foundation.org/press-room/news-archive.

Schieszler v. Ferrum College, 236 F. Supp. 2d 602 (W.D. Va. 2002).

Schmidt, P. 2009, August 25. "What's Making Colleges More Prone to Lawsuits." *Chronicle of Higher Education.* Accessed April 6, 2010. http://chronicle.com/article/Whats-Making-Colleges-More/48169.

"Virginia Tech Officials Can Be Sued Over '07 Shooting Deaths." 2010, November 23. *Roanoke Times.* Accessed November 23, 2010. http://www.roanoke.com/news/roanoke /wb/268436

Whitfield, R. N. 2003. "Managing Institutional Risks – A Framework." Unpublished doctoral dissertation, Graduate School of Education, University of Pennsylvania.

ANNE LUNDQUIST *has served as the Dean of Students at four liberal arts colleges and is currently a Doctoral Associate and PhD candidate in the Higher Education Administration program at Western Michigan University. She is the coauthor of* The Student Affairs Handbook: Translating Legal Principles into Effective Policies *(LRP Publications, 2007).*

ALLAN SHACKELFORD *is an attorney and consultant who has advised institutions of higher education for almost thirty years on various issues, including governance, accreditation, risk management, employee relations, student affairs, and disability accommodations. He has been a presenter at numerous national higher education conferences.*

NEW DIRECTIONS FOR HIGHER EDUCATION • DOI:10.1002/he

8

Student developmental theory can provide a useful framework
for understanding challenges students with disabilities may face,
providing services, and creating a welcoming campus climate.

College Students with Disabilities: A Student Development Perspective

Wanda M. Hadley

High school students with disabilities are attending colleges and universities in growing numbers, with their rate of college participation doubling in the past twenty years (Lovett and Lewandowski 2006; Wagner et al. 2005). Students with disabilities in the secondary educational system are protected by the Individuals with Disabilities Education Improvement Act (IDEIA) of 2004, which requires secondary school districts to develop special education programs and services, including a free and appropriate public education in the least restrictive environment (i.e., with a minimum of segregation from nondisabled students). In their high school experiences, students receiving special education services are supported by multidisciplinary teams available for planning and interventions related to their disabilities. Teams typically include the student, parents of the student, teachers of the student, a counselor or school psychologist, and a school administrator, who implement Individual Education Plans (IEPs) and specialized instruction.

The college environment for students with disabilities, however, does not include the same extent of support that is required in high school settings. College students with disabilities are covered by Section 504 of the Rehabilitation Act of 1973 and the Americans with Disabilities Act (ADA) of 1990 (see, e.g., AHEAD 2002; Heyward, this volume). Unlike the high school environment, however, it is the student's responsibility to initiate requests for services in the postsecondary environment. When students make the transition to higher education, they are expected to contact the Office for Students with Disabilities (OSD), self-identify as a student with a disability, provide documentation of their disability and the accommodations needed, self-advocate to their instructors, and participate in the services that will support their academic progress. Such self-advocacy moves

NEW DIRECTIONS FOR HIGHER EDUCATION, no. 154, Summer 2011 © Wiley Periodicals, Inc.
Published online in Wiley Online Library (wileyonlinelibrary.com) • DOI:10.1002/he.436

students with disabilities from a pattern of more passive dependent behavior to a more active and responsible role (Brinckerhoff, McGuire, and Shaw 2002; Hadley 2009; Hadley, Twale, and Evans 2003; Milsom and Hartley 2005). In order to successfully self-advocate, students should have a good understanding of their particular learning disability and the compensatory strategies that work best for them. Student development theory can be a useful framework to help administrators and service providers be more supportive when providing services, and to consider how the needs of students with disabilities may change throughout college.

One of the main assumptions behind serving students through the context of theory is that educational institutions are instrumental in the student's psychological and sociological development (Chickering and Reisser 1993). All newly entering students must adjust intellectually and socially to the college setting (Astin 1985; Tinto 1993), and this adjustment generally requires a degree of physical separation and emotional detachment from significant others who were important during high school, along with an acceptance of college-level expectations and rules (Schlossberg, Lynch, and Chickering 1989). These adaptations may be more challenging for students with disabilities, who often have difficulty knowing how their disability will affect them in college, including new types of testing situations and classroom instruction, social interactions, and the need to organize thoughts, information, and tasks (Brinckerhoff, McGuire, and Shaw 2002; Janiga and Costenbader 2002; Milsom and Hartley 2005). While complying with legal mandates to provide reasonable accommodations, higher education administrators may also need to assist students with disabilities in the development of their independence and self-determination skills (Brinckerhoff et al. 2002). Students are expected to manage increased levels of personal freedom, deal with the unique challenges presented by their disabilities, and to matriculate successfully into a new collegiate environment.

Individual development is a process involving the achievement of a series of developmental tasks, with specific conditions in the college environment making a difference in student development (Chickering 1969; Schlossberg, Lynch, and Chickering 1989). As adolescents become adults, they mature in intellectual skills, emotions and self-control, autonomy, identity, interpersonal relationships, career plans, and personal beliefs and values (Chickering 1969). While maturing, age, socioeconomic standing, and environmental factors can present individuals with challenges to their identity (Evans, Forney, and Guido-DiBrito 1998; Hamrick, Evans, and Schuh 2002; Evans et al. 2010), disabilities can also be a factor in development as one of the many groups of students who must work harder than others to address the academic challenges and social changes unique to the college experience (Heiman and Precel 2003; Tinto 1993). For students with disabilities, challenges can include the development of skills such as stating one's disability or discussing disability-related accommodations with professors—all strategies related to a successful transition from high school to college (Heiman and Precel 2003).

Likewise, for all students, knowing and interacting with professors may enhance students' intellectual commitment and involvement in their campus, encouraging them to think about their own values and future learning (Astin 1985). The greater the student's physical and psychological energy and involvement in the academic life of college, the greater the student's attainment of knowledge and the development of skills (Astin 1985; Tinto 1993). Highly involved students devote considerable attention to studying, spending time on campus, participating in student organizations, and interacting frequently with other students and faculty members. If successful integration and involvement does not happen, there will be a greater chance for at-risk students to feel isolated and withdraw. This is certainly applicable to students with disabilities, whose disabilities may require additional time to do daily collegiate tasks (e.g., homework, getting around campus) or their ability to interact with others, academically and socially. The Association on Higher Education And Disability (AHEAD) (2009a) has stressed the importance of students with disabilities attending college, but also the importance of their being actively encouraged to explore interests, develop their academic skills, examine life choices, pursue career opportunities, and learn to be independent individuals in an environment that encourages learning and growth—without explicit encouragement, students with disabilities may be unlikely to fully engage with their campuses.

Finally, while disabilities have been viewed traditionally as a negative characteristic addressed by disability services, it is important to consider how disabilities may become a positive aspect of students' identity (Linton 1998; Weeber 2004). Especially with the growth of disability studies and its influence on campuses (see Taylor, this volume), more students with disabilities are connecting with each other and finding ways to build communities, even if their college does not have a disability studies program. These connections can even lead to greater student activism and interest in disability issues and progressive disability services (Cory, White, and Stuckey 2010).

There are several strategies for administrators, faculty, and professionals to consider in applying developmental theory to interactions with students with disabilities:

- For students preparing for college, it is imperative that they understand the support services available to them at the school in which they are interested in attending before choosing a particular university (Milsom and Hartley 2005).
- Educators can learn more about specific disabilities of students and disability-related accommodations (e.g., extended testing times, access to printed text, physical accessibility to classrooms) through online information, health services, and disability services.

- Campuses can seek ways to implement universal design, a relatively new concept. Universally designed instruction seeks ways to create courses that are inclusive for all students from the onset (McGuire, Scott, and Shaw 2004). In this approach, the student with a disability does not have to continually advocate for access, because disabilities are seen as a naturally occurring human difference and is addressed in the same manner as other individual differences (AHEAD 2009b). Accessibility is inherently included through flexible instruction and curricula and does not need to be readdressed for each new student with a disability.
- Create connections between professionals who have a background in student development (e.g., staff in student affairs or counseling) and disability service professionals. Encourage discussions about how student development theory may influence service provision, and how knowledge of students with disabilities may enhance understanding and interpretations of developmental theory, campus diversity, and ways to improve integration and retention of students.
- Encourage cultural centers and student organizations for students with disabilities, to support connections between students with disabilities and their allies on campus. Having opportunities to build identity can help campuses feel more welcoming and provide safe places for students outside of disability services offices (Cory, White, and Stuckey 2010).
- While students with disabilities may face additional challenges in developmental tasks and their involvement on campus, supportive administrators and faculty can use developmental theory as a foundation for improving awareness and services. Campuses can be a more welcoming place when students feel safe, supported, and encouraged to grow as individuals, and their disabilities are viewed as part of the diversity of campus.

References

Association on Higher Education And Disability (AHEAD). 2002. *Section 504: The Law and Its Impact on Postsecondary Education.* Huntersville, NC: AHEAD.
———2009a. *Advising Students with Disabilities.* Huntersville, NC: AHEAD.
———2009b. *Universal Design in Higher Education: What Is Universal Design?* Huntersville, NC: AHEAD.
Astin, A. W. 1985. *Achieving Educational Excellence.* San Francisco: Jossey-Bass.
Brinckerhoff, L. C., J. M. McGuire, and S. F. Shaw. 2002. *Postsecondary Education and Transition for Students with Learning Disabilities.* 2nd ed. Austin, TX: PRO-ED.
Chickering, A. W. 1969. *Education and Identity.* San Francisco: Jossey-Bass.
Chickering, A. W., and L. Reisser. 1993. *Education and Identity.* 2nd ed. San Francisco: Jossey-Bass.
Cory, R. C., J. M. White, and Z. Stuckey. 2010. "Using Disability Studies Theory to Change Disability Services: A Case Study in Student Activism." *Journal of Postsecondary Education and Disability* 23 (1): 28–37.
Evans, N. J., D. S. Forney, and F. Guido-DiBrito. 1998. *Student Development in College: Theory, Research, and Practice.* San Francisco: Jossey-Bass.

Evans, N. J., D. S. Forney, F. M. Guido, L. D. Patton, and K. A. Renn. 2010. *Student Development in College: Theory, Research, and Practice,* 2nd ed. San Francisco: Jossey-Bass.

Hadley, W. M. 2009. "The Transition and Adjustment of First-Year Students with Specific Learning Disabilities: A Longitudinal Study." *Journal of College Orientation and Transition* 17 (1): 31–44.

Hadley, W. M., D. J. Twale, and J. H. Evans. 2003. "First-Year Students with Specific Learning Disabilities: Transition and Adjustment to Academic Expectations." *Journal of College Orientation and Transition* 11 (1): 35–46.

Hamrick, F. A., N. J. Evans, and J. H. Schuh. 2002. *Foundations of Student Affairs Practice: How Philosophy, Theory, and Research Strengthen Educational Outcomes.* San Francisco: Jossey-Bass.

Heiman, T., and K. Precel, 2003. "Students with Learning Disabilities in Higher Education: Academic Strategies Profile." *Journal of Learning Disabilities* 35 (5): 462–68, 479.

Janiga, S. J., and V. Costenbader. 2002. "The Transition from High School to Postsecondary Education for Students with Learning Disabilities: A Survey of College Service Coordinators." *Journal of Learning Disabilities* 35 (5): 462–68.

Linton, S. 1998. *Claiming Disability: Knowledge and Identity.* New York: New York University Press.

Lovett, B. J., and L. J. Lewandowski. 2006. "Gifted Students with Learning Disabilities: Who Are They?" *Journal of Learning Disabilities* 39 (6): 515–27.

McGuire, J. M., S. S. Scott, and S. F. Shaw. 2004."Universal Design for Instruction: The Paradigm, Its Principles, and Products for Enhancing Instructional Access." *Journal of Postsecondary Education and Disability* 17 (1): 10–20.

Milsom, A., and M. T. Hartley. 2005. "Assisting Students with Learning Disabilities Transitioning to College: What School Counselors Should Know." *Professional School Counseling* 8 (5): 436–41.

Schlossberg, N. K., A. Q. Lynch, and A. W. Chickering. 1989. *Improving Higher Education Environments for Adults: Responsive Programs and Services from Entry to Departure.* San Francisco: Jossey-Bass.

Tinto, V. 1993. *Leaving College: Rethinking the Causes and Cures of Student Attrition.* 2nd ed. Chicago: University of Chicago Press.

Wagner, M., L. Newman, R. Cameto, and P. Levine, 2005. *Changes Over Time in the Early Postschool Outcomes of Youth with Disabilities: A Report of Findings from the National Longitudinal Transition Study (NLTS) and the National Longitudinal Transition Study-2 (NLTS2).* Menlo Park, CA: SRI International.

Weeber, J. E. 2004. "Disability Community Leaders' Disability Identity Development: A Journey of Integration and Expansion." Unpublished doctoral dissertation, Department of Educational Research, Leadership, and Counselor Education, North Carolina State University.

Wanda M. Hadley is the Coordinator of Disability Services at Central State University and an adjunct professor in Higher Education in the College of Education. She has written extensively about the needs of first-year students with disabilities, particularly learning disabilities.

New Directions for Higher Education • DOI:10.1002/he

*Campus assessment instruments can explore the campus
climate for students, faculty, and staff with disabilities,
contributing useful insights for services and program
development.*

9

Disability-Friendly University Environments: Conducting a Climate Assessment

Robert A. Stodden, Steven E. Brown, Kelly Roberts

Introduction

What constitutes a supportive environment for all students with disabilities
in postsecondary settings? After more than ten years of collecting data
focused on the provision of educational supports to students with disabilities in postsecondary education, we have discovered numerous intervening
variables that contribute to a supportive environment. In many postsecondary situations, accommodating college environments are linked to a generalized climate of support for all students, especially those learners most
in need of accommodation and assistance. This line of inquiry led
researchers at the Center on Disability Studies (CDS) at the University of
Hawaii at Manoa to utilize and study institutional climate assessment (CA)
processes to assess the contexts related to supportive higher education settings for students and faculty with disabilities. Climate assessment is defined
as "the systematic measuring of effectiveness in an institution or program
area so that an action plan for program improvement can be created and set
in motion as a means of inducing change" (Nisonger Center 2006a, 2006b).

This climate assessment was initiated during the late 1990s by a network of national partners collaborating under the funding umbrella of the
National Center for the Study of Postsecondary Educational Supports
(NCSPES) at the University of Hawaii at Manoa (http://www.rrtc.hawaii
.edu). Further research (funded by the U.S. Department of Education's
Office of Postsecondary Education) was undertaken to explore supportive
college and university environments in an effort to inform and improve the

New Directions for Higher Education, no. 154, Summer 2011 © Wiley Periodicals, Inc.
Published online in Wiley Online Library (wileyonlinelibrary.com) • DOI:10.1002/he.437

attitudes and skills of postsecondary faculty supporting and teaching students with disabilities. These activities led to collaboration between CDS researchers and project staff from other universities to develop and pilot a range of CA instruments. As these efforts have progressed, our confidence in the promise and efficacy of CAs has deepened. We have translated their usage into other endeavors, including using a CA to survey attendee knowledge at the beginning and end of a one-day conference and the assessment of community organizations that work with volunteers with disabilities.

The authors of this chapter began exploring CA instruments, piloting their use, and developing detailed descriptions of the CA process in collaboration with the Nisonger Center at Ohio State University. CA modules were developed as part of the Faculty and Administrator Modules in Higher Education (FAME; http://www.oln.org/ILT/ada/Fame/) project (Stodden and Brown 2006a, 2006b, 2006c, 2006d). Individuals from three institutions of higher education developed and piloted a series of four CA instruments and companion instructional modules. The authors of this chapter developed the majority of the descriptive modules and collaborated with many other individuals at three institutions to produce the CA instruments. This involved numerous conference calls and a succession of drafts over a two-year period before the effort was finalized. Why expend so much effort on an institutional CA?

Why a Climate Assessment?

The term *climate assessment* may resonate with countless implications and definitions to different people and constituencies—and, in a way, that is part of its appeal. Owing to our role as a University Center on Excellence in Disability tasked to promote full community inclusion of individuals with disabilities (Association of University Centers on Disabilities [AUCD] n.d.), researchers at CDS have concentrated on disability-focused applications of CAs. In this context, we view disability, like ethnicity and gender, as a form of diversity. For many institutions, the conceptual orientation of disability as an aspect of diversity is a new concept. For this reason, it is an exciting time to evaluate how disability is perceived as a component of university life. While disability issues are the focus of the use of CAs in our work, they may be used to evaluate many other aspects of university life and institutional endeavors.

CA instruments can be utilized in a variety of settings to provide assessment and evaluative information and insight. Program or project administrators can use CAs to secure data that may reveal either the efficacy and benefit of their programs or, conversely, that these programs do not yet meet stated performance objectives and require more support and/or funding to achieve specific goals. Within higher education, meeting the preceding objectives first requires the availability of data from many sources, including faculty, students, staff, facilities personnel, admissions and records offices, research units, outreach schools, and other institutional entities tasked with specific university missions. Second, administrators must have a means to interpret data relevant to their need or purpose. Third, administrators or their institutional representatives need to report CA data in language that is accessible to their superiors and the public at large. However, once the data are collected, interpreted, and reported, administrators have the ability to develop strategic action plans to attend to problems, concerns, or inquiries suggested by the evidence, such as responsiveness to issues like student retention, resource distribution, instructional quality, support services, and the diversity of the university population.

An advantage of CA instruments is that they may be applied by academic professionals in a variety of settings and used with nearly any population or across a combination of groups such as students, faculty, staff, and facilities personnel, or any other targeted population. College deans might want to use the CAs within the context of their colleges, or within departments, or even in specific classes. Professors may also find CAs useful within their classes. CA data can be collected and refined within any of these contexts and groups to focus on a value or characteristic such as ethnicity, age, gender, and disability.

When CA instruments become part of an institutional mind-set and are well utilized, they offer great potential to enrich institutional statistics and action. From a data perspective, this might include elevating institutional data resources about student recruitment, retention, and matriculation rates, including analyzing data for specific disability groups or other selected variables, or encapsulating developments over different periods (e.g., from one to ten or more years). To stimulate action, a university might use CA evidence to ameliorate the quality of instruction, perhaps by refining existing instructional methods and curricula. Academic and other support services can also benefit from insight gleaned from a CA to resolve issues concerning access or accommodations. Another reason for using a CA is that it is a nonintrusive and efficient means of gathering and evaluating important information such as demographic data, admissions data, and class evaluations. The CA process may also be used within classes as a one-time exercise, across courses, or even within disciplines, as a foundation for institutional research studies. Understanding why and how to use a CA will help administrators and others to maximize their benefit from employing a CA.

What Is Climate Assessment Measurement and How Is It Used?

Prior to developing a CA instrument, collaborators should agree both on the specifics of what they are assessing and their objectives for undertaking the CA process and using the resulting data. So just what does *climate* mean, in the context of higher education? Giorino (1995) defines climate as:

The prevailing condition affecting life and activity. In an academic setting the climate is set by the expectations and past experiences of students, faculty members, and staff; by the history of the institution; and by the behaviors and goals that are expected and rewarded. (2)

More recent publications have offered more detailed explanations and definitions of what is meant by *climate*. In *Making Diversity Work on Campus*, Milem, Chang, and Antonio (2005) built on existing conceptual frameworks to detail and discuss racial climates on postsecondary campuses. They developed concepts that include psychological and behavioral climates as they relate to institutional structure, external forces, and ethnic or racial compositional diversity. A disability-inclusive definition of climate should include factors relating to the physical environment, accessibility of modes of teaching and learning, and available supports. For example, would a person with a learning disability have access to text in formats other than print?

Assessing institutional climates is not a simple task and requires data collection, interpretation, and comprehension around a plethora of complex issues. While a CA instrument is designed to elicit specific information during a given period of time, it is essential to understand that CA is also a dynamic process. The CA instrument may be undertaken as a stand-alone activity but may best serve as a tool within a continuum of assessment instruments and activities. Design and use of CA instruments has generally consisted of three phases of activity: preassessment (instrument development), assessment (using the instrument), and postassessment (evaluating the results of instrument responses). The following explanation details this process.

Preassessment Phase. This phase may also be viewed as the instrument development and piloting stage. Typically, a group of stakeholders assemble, either in person or via electronic communications, to develop a CA instrument. The group has a focused area of concern, such as student attitudes about and behavior toward persons with disabilities. Our own experiences within this process suggest that this phase can require significant time investments. In one instance, due to the involvement of a very diverse group of individuals and organizations representing a variety of constituencies and interests, we concluded that four different CA instruments were needed to get at the depth and breadth of data we desired. While this process required considerable time and effort, the results proved invaluable to the achievement of our assessment and evaluation objectives.

Faculty at CDS focused on the objective of developing and explaining the CA instruments to assess attitudes, physical access, and support services, while faculty at Ohio State worked on developing objectives, introductions, definitions, and case examples for the Preassessment, Assessment, Postassessment, and Institutional Data modules. Each module was piloted at our own universities and with colleagues at other universities and community colleges.

In designing the CA instruments, the cohort weighed standard survey design considerations such as time required, use of language, accessibility, and other issues. We deemed twenty questions as optimal for our collection purposes. By targeting items to specific areas of inquiry, and omitting items that did not fit our very tight focus, our instrument proved easy to complete within a reasonable amount of time. This led to high completion rates for the instrument in use and, ultimately, the collection of useful targeted data.

We refined the CA instruments by utilizing feedback garnered during piloting to better focus on our overall objectives for assessing climate relating to disability. As the attitudinal survey took shape, we used what we learned to further refine and morph three other instruments with the following focuses: programmatic supports, physical/facilities access, and instructional access. We then piloted each of these instruments and determined that we now had the CA instruments needed to achieve our goals of collecting data in a consistent manner across groups. In addition to assessment data, we collected process data to inform the undertaking of future administrations of the resulting CA instruments.

As the cohort agreed on and finalized the items to use in our CA instrument, we also developed a scoring guide for analysis of the results. After numerous discussions around design, selection, and scoring of our CA items, we decided to use an equal number of questions to which respondents could answer either "Agree" or "Disagree." We then further divided these twenty questions into subsets of four or five, refining the instrument even further as we moved into the assessment phase of this undertaking. This preassessment phase may be complex, as varying constituencies agree on what will be assessed, how and by whom these assessments will be conducted, and who will evaluate the results. However, once this was accomplished, the administration of the instrument could finally move forward.

Assessment Phase. In an effort to achieve consensus, we discussed the following variables concerning the administration of the CA instruments.

1. *Whom Do We Need to Complete the CA Instruments?* We chose to begin with our group members. Everyone involved in teaching or making presentations had opportunities to utilize the CA instrument(s), and to collect data and offer feedback to further refine the process. Participants included graduate students in classes in disability and diversity, and graduate assistants. Because we continually refined the instruments and the process, we often moved between the preassessment and assessment phases.

2. *When and How Often Should These Instruments Be Used?* This question can be responded to differently depending on the circumstances and CA process. For example, a CA instrument might be administered in a formative manner to a class at the beginning, middle, and conclusion of a semester to discern if any changes occurred during the course of

the class. In another situation, for example, a training workshop, a CA could be distributed at the beginning and end of a half-day or full-day training session.

One CDS project developed the CA instrument and scoring tool included in Exhibits 9.1 and 9.2 for a 2007 postconference of the Pacific Rim Conference on Disabilities, called "Teaching All Students, Reaching All Learners: Innovative Ways to Address Disability and Other Forms of Diversity in the Postsecondary Classroom." We modified this instrument to include only ten items so that it could be completed and scored quickly. Before using the instrument at the workshop, we piloted it internally at CDS and refined it based on staff feedback. Each of these questions had a specific goal: to lead to an understanding of the audience. This information was then used to divide the audience into groups to work on issues of disability accommodation provision, universal design for instruction, and faculty support provision.

3. *Who Will Collect the Information?* This discussion will probably already have occurred during the preassessment phase. During the assessment process, the individual or office responsible for supervising, collecting, and evaluating the data will need to be identified and have the resources to achieve this task. After data collection is complete, the data will be delivered to the party accountable for analyzing them, which triggers the postassessment phase.

Exhibit 9.1. Climate Assessment

| I am a(n): | _____ Instructor/Faculty | _____ Administrator |
| | _____ Support Person | _____ Student |

Using the rating scale provided below, place an "A" for Agree or a "D" for Disagree in each space provided to indicate your agreement or disagreement with the statement. Please respond to each item and complete the survey honestly and thoroughly. Thank you for your time and patience.

A = Agree   D = Disagree

1. _____ Students with disabilities are responsible for initiating conferences with instructors to discuss accommodations in a college class.
2. _____ Instructors should know how to differentiate teaching styles, materials, and methods to assist students with diverse learning styles to learn in their classes.
3. _____ Students with disabilities are responsible for obtaining their own accommodations to use library computers.
4. _____ Many environmental and societal conditions prevent students with disabilities from participating in extracurricular activities the same as all other students.
5. _____ Faculty and/or students without disabilities might resent it when a student with a disability uses a notetaker that other students are not allowed use.
6. _____ It is not the responsibility of individual professors to be aware of the different accommodations available for students with various disability needs who are in their classrooms.

(Continued)

Exhibit 9.1. (*Continued*)

7. _____ Students with disabilities should be addressed in the classroom in exactly the same way as all other students who need assistance to learn.
8. _____ Instructors are responsible for making the content they teach accessible to all students in their class regardless of their special needs.
9. _____ Faculty offices should be universally accessible and open to all students regardless of their learning, physical, or mobility needs.
10. _____ Students with disabilities should have the same opportunity as all other students to take online courses.

Exhibit 9.2. Climate Assessment: 2007 CBI Scoring Guide

This instrument is intended to survey attitudes of persons in postsecondary education (administrators, faculty, staff, and students) toward typical situations involving students with disabilities. The instrument seeks to measure how respondents (including persons with disabilities) perceive ten different situations routinely encountered within postsecondary education environments. Respondents are asked to agree or disagree, individually, with each of the ten items below.

In scoring this rating scale it is important for the person charged with this task to note that each of the ten items in the instrument has been identified with either a positive (+) or a negative (−) value. There are an equal number of items assigned to a negative and positive value (five each). Those items coded with a plus reflect positively on the campus attitudinal climate toward persons with disabilities; those coded as a minus reflect the reverse or a more negative campus attitudinal climate.

Steps for Scoring and Interpretation. Possible responses to items are "Agree" or "Disagree." The following steps are required to score and interpret the results:

1. The first step in scoring this instrument is to understand the relationship between the plus and minus values assigned to the items (noted below for each item) and the response (Agree or Disagree) provided by the person completing the instrument. If the item has been assigned a negative value and the response is "Disagree," then one point is scored for the item. If the response to an item has been assigned a negative value and the response is "Agree," then no point is scored for the item. If an item has been assigned a positive value and the response is "Agree," then one point is scored for the item; if the response is "Disagree," then no point is scored for the item. Also, if the item is left blank, no point is given.

2. The second step in scoring is to add up the number of points given responses for each instrument—the range of points possible for a single instrument should be between 0 and 10, with 5 being a midrange score. The closer the point total for an individual instrument is to 10, the greater the indication of an overall positive attitudinal climate toward persons with disabilities on campus.

3. The third step in scoring is to average the point totals for all completed instruments or for subgroupings of respondents (faculty, students, administrators, or other categories), depending on the goal of the instrument administrator. This step is completed by adding up the totals for all instruments completed (or grouped together) and then dividing that total by the number of instruments used in the averaging process. This should give you an average for scores across a total set of instruments or a specific group of respondents.

(*Continued*)

Exhibit 9.2. (*Continued*)

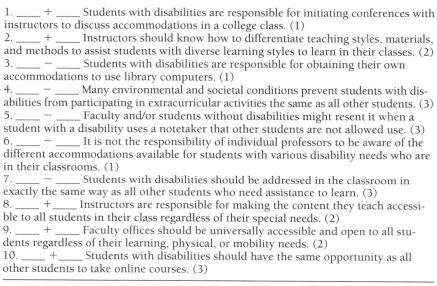

4. When interpreting data from this scoring process, averages closer to 7–10 indicate a positive attitudinal climate on campus; averages that drop below 5 provide an indication that a negative attitudinal climate may be present on campus.

Value Coding of Items. Each item on this instrument is worded in a positive or negative manner and has been assigned a value, as follows:

1. ____ + ____ Students with disabilities are responsible for initiating conferences with instructors to discuss accommodations in a college class. (1)

2. ____ + ____ Instructors should know how to differentiate teaching styles, materials, and methods to assist students with diverse learning styles to learn in their classes. (2)

3. ____ − ____ Students with disabilities are responsible for obtaining their own accommodations to use library computers. (1)

4. ____ − ____ Many environmental and societal conditions prevent students with disabilities from participating in extracurricular activities the same as all other students. (3)

5. ____ − ____ Faculty and/or students without disabilities might resent it when a student with a disability uses a notetaker that other students are not allowed use. (3)

6. ____ − ____ It is not the responsibility of individual professors to be aware of the different accommodations available for students with various disability needs who are in their classrooms. (1)

7. ____ − ____ Students with disabilities should be addressed in the classroom in exactly the same way as all other students who need assistance to learn. (3)

8. ____ + ____ Instructors are responsible for making the content they teach accessible to all students in their class regardless of their special needs. (2)

9. ____ + ____ Faculty offices should be universally accessible and open to all students regardless of their learning, physical, or mobility needs. (2)

10. ____ + ____ Students with disabilities should have the same opportunity as all other students to take online courses. (3)

Postassessment Phase. Perhaps the most significant aspect of the postassessment process is deciding who will interpret the data. As it happened, one member of our group had undertaken CAs as part of her dissertation, to determine how well students with psychological disabilities were supported in different types of academic programs, including classroom settings, compared to clinical or internship program settings. Since the instrument development process (preassessment phase) and the data collection (assessment phase) were part of her dissertation data, it was convenient for her to conduct an analysis of the data and report it out as a part of her overall study (Casey 2006). The research findings indicated that professional development opportunities are needed for faculty and staff to improve the academic climate for students with psychological disabilities (Casey 2006). In addition, "positive attitudinal indicators, increased support provisions, and frequent student interactions between faculty, staff, and students were found to be key indicators for student academic success" (Casey 2006, v).

The authors' findings, when utilizing a CA as part of a pre- and postworkshop assessment to determine change in participants' attitudes and perceptions, are in support of the findings from Casey (2006). The topics of this workshop were universal design for learning, hidden disabilities in postsecondary education, and assistive technology in postsecondary education. The workshop participants indicated that completing the CA, in and of itself, influenced a positive change in their attitudes and perceptions. In addition, the participants indicated that the pre-CA helped them "immediately" apply the content of the workshop while considering their perceptions and thus adjust them based on the information presented in the workshop.

While the authors and partners involved in the development of the CAs were in a position to analyze the data and report back to the "subjects" in most higher education settings, an Office of Institutional Research would be charged with analyzing and reporting data collected (as currently occurs with student course evaluations in many universities). The postassessment phase should also include discussions to determine where the data will be kept and how different audiences will have access to it. Storage of the actual documents might occur in an administrative office, a library, or a departmental office. In any case, methods for researchers and other interested parties to access the information need to be considered. One possibility would be to share the information via a website. Sharing the data makes sense, since the purpose of the CA process is both to assess current conditions and to stimulate change. Finally, because the CA is a dynamic process, the postassessment stage is most likely to lead directly into the next phase of preassessment instrument planning and another round of data collection.

Conclusion

In university settings there are many benefits to using a CA. One of the most valuable is use by faculty involved in program development, as demonstrated by Casey (2006). Other benefits of CAs may be related to accommodations. This could include (1) informing faculty about the existence and different types of accommodations, (2) differentiating between how students and staff perceive accommodations and their use, (3) thinking creatively about providing accommodations, and (4) determining where and how to implement accommodations.

In addition, CAs can help assess differences including diverse learning needs, styles, and cultures. The dynamic process of CAs and possibly resulting change in program delivery can assist faculty in understanding their own biases and preconceptions and has the potential to ameliorate the teaching and learning experience—for everyone involved.

References

Association of University Centers on Disabilities (AUCD). Homepage. Accessed November 27, 2006. http://www.aucd.org/aucd_aboutuce.htm.

Casey, D. A. 2006. "Indicators Linked to the Success of Students with Psychological Dis-
    abilities in Urban Community College Allied Health Sciences Programs." Unpublished
    doctoral dissertation, College of Education, Florida Atlantic University.
Giorino, A. B. 1995. *Warming the Climate for Women in Academic Science.* Washington,
    DC: Association of American Colleges and Universities/PSEW.
Milem, J. F., M. J. Chang, and A. L. Antonio. 2005. *Making Diversity Work on Campus:
    A Research-Based Perspective.* Washington, DC: Association of American Colleges and
    Universities.
Nisonger Center, Ohio State University. 2006a. "'Frequently Asked Questions.' Climate
    Assessment in Higher Education." Columbus: Faculty and Administrator Modules in
    Higher Education (FAME) Project, Ohio State University. Accessed August 18, 2010.
    http://www.oln.org/ILT/ada/Fame/ca/faq5.html.
————2006b. "Climate Assessment in Higher Education." Columbus: Faculty and
    Administrator Modules in Higher Education (FAME) Project, Ohio State University.
    Accessed November 17, 2007. http://www.oln .org/ILT/ada/Fame/.
Stodden, R. A., and S. E. Brown. 2006a, "Climate Assessment Instrument #1: Attitudes."
    Columbus: Ohio State University Faculty and Administrator Modules in Higher Edu-
    cation (FAME) Project, Ohio State University. Accessed April 6, 2007.
    http://www.oln.org/ILT/ada/Fame/.
————2006b. "Climate Assessment Instrument #2: Programmatic Supports." Colum-
    bus: Ohio State University Faculty and Administrator Modules in Higher Education
    (FAME) Project, Ohio State University. Accessed April 6, 2007. http://www
    .oln.org/ILT/ada/Fame/.
————2006c. "Climate Assessment Instrument #3: Physical/Facilities Access." Colum-
    bus: Ohio State University Faculty and Administrator Modules in Higher Education
    (FAME) Project, Ohio State University. Accessed April 6, 2007. http://www
    .oln.org/ILT/ada/Fame/.
————2006d. "Climate Assessment Instrument #4: Instructional Access." Columbus:
    Ohio State University Faculty and Administrator Modules in Higher Education
    (FAME) Project, Ohio State University. Accessed April 6, 2007. http://www
    .oln.org/ILT/ada/Fame/.

ROBERT A. STODDEN *is the Director of the Center on Disability Studies and Professor of Special Education at the University of Hawaii at Manoa, and a past
president of the Association of University Centers on Disabilities.*

STEVEN E. BROWN *is an Associate Professor and Disabilities Scholar at the Center on Disability Studies at the University of Hawaii at Manoa and cofounder
of the Institute on Disability Culture.*

KELLY ROBERTS *is a Project Director and Associate Professor at the Center on Disability Studies at the University of Hawaii at Manoa, where she directs the CDS
Pacific Outreach Initiative.*

10

Disability studies courses and programs can have a positive and transformative effect on disability services, students with disabilities, and the broader campus climate by placing disability issues in social, cultural, and political context.

Disability Studies in Higher Education

Steven J. Taylor

Every new group entering higher education has a profound influence on academic programs and curricula. The expansion of educational opportunities for women and members of ethnic minorities since the 1960s led to the establishment of programs in women's and gender studies, African American Studies, Latino Studies, Native American Studies, and similar ethnic studies. More recently, the gay and lesbian rights movement and the increased acceptance of lesbian, gay, bisexual, and transgender (LGBT) persons in American society has resulted in the emergence of LGBT programs at many colleges and universities. The latest group to increase its presence on American campuses is students with disabilities. In 1975, the passage of P.L. 94–142, later renamed the Individuals with Disabilities Education Act, increased opportunities for students with disabilities in America's schools and raised expectations of people with disabilities that they could benefit from educational programs and contribute to society. The Americans with Disabilities Act, passed in 1990, required educational institutions, as well as other public and private entities, to end discrimination against people with disabilities. As increasing numbers of students with disabilities have entered higher education, it is only natural that they would expect universities and colleges to develop academic programs that reflect their experiences in society.

As a topic of study, disability is not new at institutions of higher education. Psychological and intellectual disabilities have been of interest in psychiatry and psychology at least since the late 1800s and early 1900s. The post–World War II era, in particular, witnessed the rapid expansion of academic programs in special education, vocational rehabilitation, speech and language disorders, and similar clinical or instructional areas. In sociology, courses in social problems and deviance have covered disability, along with race, ethnicity, and sexuality, since the early part of the twentieth century.

NEW DIRECTIONS FOR HIGHER EDUCATION, no. 154, Summer 2011 © Wiley Periodicals, Inc.
Published online in Wiley Online Library (wileyonlinelibrary.com) • DOI:10.1002/he.438

Each of these fields views disability from the perspective of a nondisabled majority. Disability has been treated as a condition to be cured or ameliorated or a characteristic that can interfere with the social order and social interaction. Enter disability studies.

The academic area of disability studies approaches disability from a different vantage point than traditional fields. It examines disability as a social, cultural, and political phenomenon. In contrast to clinical, medical, instructional, or therapeutic perspectives on disability, Disability Studies focuses on how disability is defined and represented in society. From this perspective, disability is not a characteristic that exists exclusively in the person so defined, but a construct that finds its meaning in social and cultural context. This is similar to the way in which women's and gender studies approaches the difference between *sex* as a biological condition and *gender* as a social role.

Disability Studies is a vibrant and diverse field or area of scholarly inquiry. First, it is interdisciplinary and multidisciplinary. No single academic discipline can place a claim on Disability Studies. Rather, the field is informed by scholarship from such different disciplines as history, sociology, literature, philosophy, political science, law, policy studies, economics, cultural studies, anthropology, geography, theology, communications and media studies, and the arts. Major professional associations, including the Modern Language Association, the American Sociological Association, the American Education Research Association, and the American Studies Association, have interest groups on Disability Studies.

Second, Disability Studies covers an incredibly diverse group of people. People who are blind, deaf, use wheelchairs, have chronic pain or fatigue, learn at a slower pace than other people, process written words differently from others, and so on, have vastly different experiences and perspectives. Does it make sense to lump together such different human beings under the category of disability? It does—not because they are the same in any biological or philosophical sense, but because society has placed them in this category, with consequences for how they are viewed and treated by the majority presumed to be nondisabled.

Finally, it is easier to define what Disability Studies is *not* (medicine; rehabilitation; special education; speech and language disorders; and professions oriented toward the cure, prevention, or treatment of disabilities) than to specify what it *is*. Although Disability Studies scholars generally subscribe to the "minority group model" of disability—the view that the status of people as a minority shapes their experiences in society—they can agree on little else. Some scholars view disability in terms of culture and identity, while others regard disability as a label and social construct. Others consider disability as both an identity and a social construct. Further, Disability Studies scholars differ on the compatibility of Disability Studies with other academic perspectives on disability. Some reject medical and clinical approaches to disability and argue that these approaches inherently treat disability as pathological. Others maintain that different perspectives on disability can coexist, with Disability Studies bringing much-needed attention to society's treatment of people with disabilities.

Scholars even use different language to refer to the people at the center of inquiry in disability. *Disabled person* is used to draw attention to the centrality of disability in individual identity; *person with a disability* or *people first language* conveys the idea that having a disability is secondary to people's identities as human beings; *person labeled disabled* (*mentally retarded, intellectually disabled, mentally ill,* and so on) focuses on how disability is a socially constructed definition imposed on people. Within different groups, minor variations in language and spelling can carry tremendous significance. Thus, *deaf person* and *Deaf person* mean very different things, with the latter emphasizing membership in a linguistic minority, based on the use of American Sign Language.

The first Disability Studies programs in the United States were established in the mid-1990s. Today, there are at least twenty-nine undergraduate and graduate disability studies programs in the country, with one or two additional programs added every year. Table 10.1 provides a listing of universities or colleges that offer undergraduate or graduate degrees, minors, majors, or certificates in Disability Studies.[1] The Society for Disability Studies and the Disability Studies in Education group, which is associated with the American Education Research Association, sponsor annual Disability Studies conferences. Major academic publishers, including New York University Press, Syracuse University Press, Temple University Press, and the University of Michigan Press, have Disability Studies series or have published multiple titles in Disability Studies. Although Disability Studies scholarship can be found in many social science, humanities, policy, and applied journals, the *Disability Studies Quarterly*, *Disability and Society*, and the *Journal of Disability Policy Studies* are exclusively devoted to disability studies work.

Disability Studies is an academic area of inquiry, not a service field. Colleges and universities are required to provide accommodations to students, faculty, and staff with disabilities under Section 504 of the Rehabilitation Act of 1973 and the Americans with Disabilities Act, and most maintain offices of disability services. Although Disability Studies programs do not provide services to students with disabilities, they can complement offices of disability services and help to make campus culture more inclusive and accepting of students with disabilities. Accommodations provided in compliance with the law are important, but cannot change attitudinal barriers that can isolate and marginalize students with disabilities. Just as women's and gender studies, African American, and LGBT studies programs have influenced college or university policies and practices, Disability Studies programs can address issues that transcend in-class accommodations.

Disability Studies is well established in higher education. The question that arises is: Why should colleges and universities support disability studies programs? Disability is part of the human condition and will touch practically

Table 10.1. U.S. Academic Programs in Disability Studies

Academic Institution	Program	Academic Unit
California Baptist University	Master of Arts in Disability Studies	School of Education
Chapman University	PhD in Education, Disability Studies Emphasis	Academic Unit: College of Educational Studies
City University of New York	Master of Arts in Disability Studies	CUNY School of Professional Studies
	Multidisciplinary Graduate Certificate in Disability Studies	
College of Staten Island, City University of New York	Minor in Disability Studies, Interdisciplinary Program	Department of Sociology, Anthropology, and Social Work
Eastern Washington University	Certificate in Disability Studies	Center for Disability Studies and Universal Access
	Graduate Certificate in Disability Studies	
Gallaudet University	Master of Arts in Deaf Studies	Department of American Sign Language (ASL) and Deaf Studies
	Cultural Studies Concentration	
	Deaf History Concentration	
	Sign Language Teaching Concentration	
Hofstra University	Disability Studies Program (Undergraduate Minor)	College of Liberal Arts and Sciences
Miami University	Undergraduate Disability Studies Minor	College of Arts and Sciences
National-Louis University	Disability and Equity in Education Doctoral Program	National College of Education
Northern Arizona University	Undergraduate Minor in Disability Studies	College of Social and Behavioral Sciences
Ohio State University	Undergraduate Minor in Disability Studies	Arts and Sciences (Interdisciplinary)
	Graduate Interdisciplinary Specialization in Disability Studies	
Pacific University	Disability Studies in the Humanities and Social Sciences (Minor)	College of Arts and Sciences
Stony Brook University	Disabilities Studies Concentration, Bachelor of Science in Health Science	School of Health Technology and Management
Syracuse University	Graduate (Master's and PhD)	Cultural Foundations of Education, School of Education
	Graduate Certificate of Advanced Study (CAS) Science in Health Science	
	Joint Degree Program in Law (JD) and Education (Master's and CAS in Disability Studies); Undergraduate Minor in Disability Studies	

University	Program	College/Department
Teachers College, Columbia University	Disability Studies in Education, Concentration in the EdD Program in Curriculum and Teaching	Department of Curriculum and Teaching, College of Education
Temple University	Graduate Certificate in Disability Studies	
Washington State University	Undergraduate Minor in Disability Studies	Department of Speech and Hearing Sciences
University of California at Berkeley	Minor in Disability Studies in Undergraduate Interdisciplinary Studies	Undergraduate and Interdisciplinary Studies
University of California at Los Angeles (UCLA)	Undergraduate Disability Studies Minor	Division of Undergraduate Education, College of Letters and Science
University of Delaware	Undergraduate Interdisciplinary Minor in Disabilities Studies	College of Education and Human Development
University of Hawaii at Manoa	Interdisciplinary Certificate in Disability and Diversity Studies	Center on Disability Studies and Educational Foundations
University of Illinois at Chicago	PhD in Disability Studies; Master of Science in Disability and Human Development	Department of Disability and Human Development; College of Applied Health Sciences
University of Maine	Minor in Interdisciplinary Disability Studies and Graduate Interdisciplinary Concentration in Disability Studies	Center for Community Inclusion and Disability Studies
University of Massachusetts–Lowell	Undergraduate Disability Studies Minor	College of Arts and Sciences
University of Pittsburgh	Graduate Disability Studies Certificate Program	School of Health and Rehabilitation Sciences, Department of Health Information Management
University of Toledo	Undergraduate Interdisciplinary Minor in Disability Studies; Master of Liberal Studies Program (MLS), Concentration in Disability Studies (DST)	College of Arts and Sciences
University of Washington	Individualized Studies Major in Disability Studies	College of Arts and Sciences
University of Wisconsin–Madison	Interdisciplinary Cluster	College of Letters and Science*
University of Wyoming	Minor in Disability Studies	College of Health Sciences

* The University of Wisconsin–Madison does not yet have a formal academic program in Disability Studies. However, the university has made a commitment to the development of a program through a cluster hiring initiative to fill multiple tenure-track positions in Disability Studies.

all students directly or indirectly at some time in their lives. If people live long enough, they will either become disabled or have a family member or close friend experience a disability. For students with disabilities, in particular, Disability Studies can help them understand their personal experiences in social, cultural, and political context. From a scholarly standpoint, disability provides an intellectual lens through which to examine everything ranging from cultural conceptions of beauty or normality to the social dynamics of stereotyping, discrimination, and exclusion. Many, if not most, colleges and universities offer degrees in vocational rehabilitation, special education, and other applied fields. Students in social work, child and family development, and related fields often take disability-related courses. For students in applied fields, Disability Studies courses can complement their programs of study and help them understand that the best instructional and clinical interventions will be undermined if children and adults with disabilities continue to face social, physical, and attitudinal barriers to their full participation in society.

By developing Disability Studies programs, colleges and universities can demonstrate their commitment to diversity and, based on the experience at Syracuse University and elsewhere, strengthen their student recruitment efforts. Prospective undergraduate and graduate students who have disabilities or have a family member or sibling with disabilities are likely to be attracted to a minor, certificate, or degree program in Disability Studies. Graduate students who pursue Disability Studies programs also include those who have held positions in special education, vocational rehabilitation, or other helping professionals and have become disillusioned by societal or administrative obstacles to their students' or clients' inclusion in society. Undergraduates in Disability Studies programs often have had a volunteer or personal experience that draws them to the area of disability. So having a Disability Studies program enables colleges and universities to communicate to prospective students: "If you want to pursue a degree in sociology, literature, history, education, social work, or other disciplines, but also have a personal or professional interest in the area of disability, our college or university is the right one for you." Disability studies can enrich campus life, college or university curricula, and the diverse composition of the student body.

Note

1. This listing is based on a review of curricula and courses offered at these colleges and universities to ensure that they incorporate disability studies content.

Steven J. Taylor is the Coordinator and Centennial Professor of Disability Studies and Director of the Center on Human Policy, Law, and Disability Studies at Syracuse University.

New Directions for Higher Education • DOI:10.1002/he

INDEX

ORDER FORM SUBSCRIPTION AND SINGLE ISSUES

DISCOUNTED BACK ISSUES:

Use this form to receive 20% off all back issues of *New Directions for Higher Education*.
All single issues priced at **$23.20** (normally $29.00)

TITLE	ISSUE NO.	ISBN

Call 888-378-2537 or see mailing instructions below. When calling, mention the promotional code JBNND to receive your discount. For a complete list of issues, please visit www.josseybass.com/go/ndhe

SUBSCRIPTIONS: (1 YEAR, 4 ISSUES)

☐ New Order   ☐ Renewal

U.S.	☐ Individual: $89	☐ Institutional: $259
CANADA/MEXICO	☐ Individual: $89	☐ Institutional: $299
ALL OTHERS	☐ Individual: $113	☐ Institutional: $333

Call 888-378-2537 or see mailing and pricing instructions below.
Online subscriptions are available at www.onlinelibrary.wiley.com

ORDER TOTALS:

Issue / Subscription Amount: $ _____

Shipping Amount: $ _____
(for single issues only – subscription prices include shipping)

Total Amount: $ _____

SHIPPING CHARGES:	
First Item	$5.00
Each Add'l Item	$3.00

(No sales tax for U.S. subscriptions. Canadian residents, add GST for subscription orders. Individual rate subscriptions must be paid by personal check or credit card. Individual rate subscriptions may not be resold as library copies.)

BILLING & SHIPPING INFORMATION:

☐ **PAYMENT ENCLOSED:** *(U.S. check or money order only. All payments must be in U.S. dollars.)*

☐ **CREDIT CARD:**   ☐ VISA   ☐ MC   ☐ AMEX

Card number _____ Exp. Date _____

Card Holder Name _____ Card Issue # _____

Signature _____ Day Phone _____

☐ **BILL ME:** *(U.S. institutional orders only. Purchase order required.)*

Purchase order # _____
　　　　　　　　　Federal Tax ID 13559302 • GST 89102-8052

Name _____

Address _____

Phone _____ E-mail _____

Copy or detach page and send to:　**John Wiley & Sons, PTSC, 5th Floor**
　　　　　　　　　　　　　　　　　989 Market Street, San Francisco, CA 94103-1741

Order Form can also be faxed to:　**888-481-2665**

PROMO JBNND